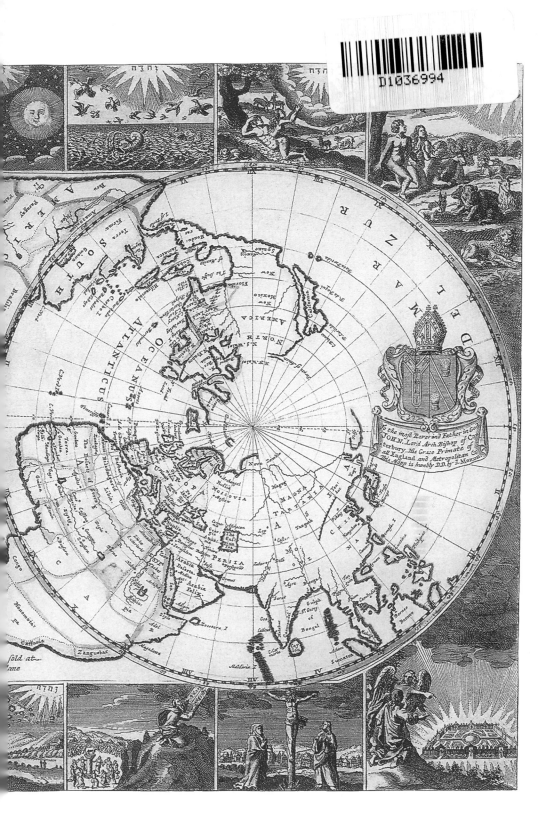

*for Mary Kathy —
who made it all happen!*

BROTHER
ASTRONOMER

Guy Consolmagno SJ

Cranbrook Oct 2000

Other books by
BROTHER GUY CONSOLMAGNO

The Way to the Dwelling of Light
Turn Left at Orion *with Dan Davis*
Worlds Apart *with Martha Schaefer*
Cosmic Pinball, *contributor*

BROTHER ASTRONOMER

ADVENTURES OF A VATICAN SCIENTIST

Brother Guy Consolmagno SJ

VATICAN OBSERVATORY

McGraw-Hill

New York San Francisco Washington, D.C. Auckland Bogotá
Caracas Lisbon London Madrid Mexico City Milan
Montreal New Delhi San Juan Singapore
Sydney Tokyo Toronto

McGraw-Hill

A Division of The **McGraw·Hill** Companies

1 2 3 4 5 6 7 8 9 0   DOC/DOC   0 9 8 7 6 5 4 3 2 1 0

ISBN 0-07-135428-X

This book was set in Aldine by North Market Street Graphics.
Printed and bound by R. R. Donnelley & Sons Company.

McGraw-Hill books are available at special quantity discounts to use as premiums
and sales promotions, or for use in corporate training programs. For more
information, please write to the Director of Special Sales, Professional Publishing,
McGraw-Hill, Two Penn Plaza, New York, NY 10121-2298. Or contact your local
bookstore.

 This book is printed on recycled, acid-free paper containing a minimun of 50% recycled, de-inked fiber.

CONTENTS

Contents

PART FOUR

WIDE WILD WHITENESS

AFTERWORD

Introduction:
A Day in the Life

The Missing Mass Problem

The noise outside my window wakes me up even before the alarm has had a chance to go off. Workers happily shouting to each other in Italian are dragging a hundred chairs out into the courtyard below my room. In an hour, the chairs will be filled by a group of nuns from Poland, singing their hearts out at the Pope's Mass. Grumbling at the noise, I stumble out of bed and into the shower.

Daily Mass for me is at 7 a.m. Our chapel here in the Jesuit community of the Vatican Observatory overlooks the courtyard where the Pope presides; we want to be finished before he starts, so that we don't have to compete with the singing that fills the whole palace. Most of the year, our quarters here in the Alban Hills south of Rome are quiet and almost deserted. But for 2 months, mid-July through September, they're filled with activity as the Pope comes to escape the summer heat of Rome.

Mass is in Italian. Working in a foreign language, even the language of my great grandfather, is still a challenge for my American ears. But I'm bilingual in another sense as well. I'm an astronomer, with degrees from the Massachusetts Institute of Technology (MIT) and the University of Arizona, and for 25 years I've worked and conversed with fellow planetary astronomers. For the last 10 years, I've also been a Jesuit brother, a student of the spiritual exercises of St. Ignatius, conversant with the terms—and concerns—of the theologians.

Some people are surprised that the Vatican supports an astronomical observatory. *The Chicago Tribune* (the same paper that declared "Dewey Defeats Truman" in 1948) once suggested we were the Pope's astrologers who set the date of Easter every year. The *Weekly World News* thinks we're training to be missionaries to Martians. A late-night radio talk show has suggested we're behind the conspiracy to cover up the truth behind UFOs!

But, in fact, astronomy was part of the original seven subjects of the medieval universities, and those universities were themselves founded by the Church. The "father of geology" who first described and classified minerals was the Dominican monk known today as Albert the Great. The "father of astrophysics" who first classified stars by their spectra was a Jesuit, Angelo Secchi. The modern big bang theory originated with a twentieth-century priest, Georges Lemaître.

The Vatican had a direct practical interest in supporting astronomical research when it reformed the calendar in 1582—a work headed by the Jesuit mathematician Christopher Clavius. There's a prominent crater on the Moon named for him (as fans of the movie *2001: A Space Odyssey* will recall) along with two dozen other craters named for Jesuit astronomers. No surprise; the fellow who drew the map and named the craters, the basis of all our modern Moon maps, was himself the Jesuit priest Francesco Grimaldi. (He also invented the wave theory of light.)

And yet, this mass of religious tradition at the heart of our science is something many people completely miss.

The Correspondence Principle

Climbing the stairs to my office, I wonder if any Jesuits were involved with the invention of e-mail. If so, I'm not sure I'd thank them.

I spend half my year living and working at the Specola Vaticana headquarters in the Papal Palace at Castel Gandolfo; half my year at the Vatican Observatory Research Group in Tucson, Arizona, affiliated with the Steward Observatory of the University of Arizona; and half my year on the road. (And I've begun to notice that the year isn't long enough to support a schedule like this . . .) The Internet both keeps me connected to my colleagues at the University of Arizona and gets in my way as it fills my time with fires to put out. Thanks to the 9-hour time difference, my American friends have been busy e-mailing me all night. Now, first thing in the morning, I have dozens of messages to answer.

Dan Britt is proposing to the National Aeronautics and Space Administration (NASA) a new Discovery-class mission to an asteroid. What instruments would I like to see flown? Bill Hubbard is checking on his CCD camera, which we used last week on our 24-inch telescope here to observe Pluto passing in front of a faint star. Larry Lebofsky has questions concerning the upcoming meeting of the American Astronomical Society (AAS), Division for Planetary Sciences. All interesting stuff, but too little of it is related to my primary research interest in the physical evolution of meteorites.

The Vatican has one of the largest meteorite collections in the world. It was the donation of a French nobleman, the Marquis de Mauroy, one of the premier meteorite collectors of the nineteenth century. Originally, astronomers at the Vatican Observatory hoped to take spectra of these space rocks; from the 1930s to the 1960s the Observatory boasted one of the best spectrochemical laboratories in the world, cataloging the spectral lines of the metallic elements. They never got around to measuring meteorites, though, which was just as well. It turns out that the most diagnostic spectral features for meteorites are in infrared wavelengths that require detectors that were unavailable back then.

More e-mail relates to those meteorites and my job as their curator. A collector in Texas is proposing a trade. A prospector in Arizona has generously offered me a piece of a recent find. Monica Grady, curator at the British Museum of Natural History, is arranging for me to have thin sections made in their lab.

I have an "in" there, in London. Not only are Monica and I old friends, but her assistant, Sara Russell, was a camp mate of mine during the 1996 meteorite hunting expedition in Antarctica. Speaking of Antarctica, on my desk is a letter from Keizo Yanai, the Japanese inventor of Antarctic meteorite hunting, looking to borrow a piece of a meteorite from Mars.

London, Japan, Antarctica, Tucson, Rome . . . will some future colleague of mine make it into space? Father George Coyne, our director, applied for astronaut training back in the 1960s. (His provincial approved, but only after muttering, "If I let you become an astronaut, George, then everyone will want to . . .") A Jesuit's vocation is to travel.

Next to the Vatican itself, the Jesuits may be the most misunderstood religious group in the world. We're neither as good, nor as bad, as they say. Famous as theologians, philosophers, poets, artists, scientists, Jesuits go through more years of education than any other order. And our mission of high school and university education puts that learning on public display. But it's more than just the education that makes us scholars. Our study is our worship: our charism (as the theologians like to say) is "to find God in all things."

Galilean Relativity

I look at the pile of work on my desk, and the unanswered e-mail messages, and ask myself, is this any different from what I was doing as a physics professor, before I entered the Jesuits?

And there's more e-mail downloading. A prominent fantasy writer (and friend of mine), P. C. Hodgell, is setting her latest book in medieval England; she wants to know about liturgical practices of the fourteenth century. I'm the closest she can come to an "expert" in Church things. Maybe I know who to ask? I don't, but I know who to ask to find out who to ask. Recreating the medieval world can be a tricky topic, but I admire her work, and I trust her to "get it right."

By contrast, I think of another novel I've just finished reading, whose fantasy universe portrays the Church as the evil suppressor of wonderful, powerful pre-Christian forces. Much as I love reading fantasy and science fiction, the Christian in me gets tired of being cast as the heavy. And the logical scientist in me wonders, if paganism was so wonderful and so powerful, then how did Christianity ever triumph in the western world? That author had no good answer for her fantasy universe. I wonder if she's ever worked it out for the real world?

I sigh. "Everybody knows" about witch hunts and inquisitions, Galileo and Bruno and Darwin. But I wonder how many people have actually taken the time to look into those histories in detail? Would an atheist's "faith" in the evils of religion survive the shock if he or she should ever learn what really went on back then?

Science and Christianity—Judaism and Islam, too—have an intimate tie. Without faith in a Creator God, one who looks at His universe and declares it good, how can you justify the belief that this universe is worth studying . . . indeed, that the universe even makes enough sense to be able to be studied? Paganism didn't have that. Pagans could make calendars; they couldn't ask the deeper questions, like why calendars should work in the first place.

Another friend, an engineer, writes: "My mother, a devout Presbyterian, is also a big fan of the Pope. She's dying of cancer. Can you arrange a Papal blessing for her?" The great rites of passage—birth, marriage, death—all call on religion. I'm happy to serve as a conduit, a "friend in the business." And I've long since gotten over the surprise of seeing Protestants honor my Church. After all, it's mutual. My favorite writers, Lewis and L'Engle, Buechner and Bonhoffer, cover a spectrum of faiths. Billy Graham and Desmond Tutu are *my* heroes, too. Though there are certainly places where we'd still disagree, here in the trenches we know that it's the same Spirit working in us all.

But my own spirit is flagging. It's nearly nine o'clock now, I've been at my computer for an hour and a half, and I've only just finished going through the mail.

I spend the next hour working on a spreadsheet, gathering data on meteorite densities. In our library I have found a collection of papers compiled in 1915 with descriptions and measurements of every meteorite fall in North America during the nineteenth century. We have samples of many of those meteorites in our collection downstairs; by comparing present values with those in this compilation, I hope to get a feel for how terrestrial weathering has altered the fabric of meteorites . . . and, maybe, how I can correct for that weathering.

Dark Matter as a Catalyst for Information Exchange

Ten o'clock, and a chime on my computer wakes me up. It's time for coffee. There's an industrial-strength cappuccino machine in our kitchen, and a number of Italians who really know how to use it.

But more than just a break, this is the one time all of us get to gather and talk about the work. Italian flows freely, with accents ranging from Naples (Sabino Maffeo) to Padua (Alessandro Omizzolo), Spain (Juan Casanovas) to Britain (Chris Corbally), New England (Rich Boyle) to California (Bill Stoeger), Argentina (José Funes) to Brazil (Mario Magalhaes—not a Jesuit, but visiting this month with his family from São Paulo). Our staff is small and informal, but very international.

Bill, who does general relativity, is talking with Alessandro about the next conference in a series we've sponsored with the Center for Theology and the Natural Sciences at Berkeley. The theme is "Divine Action in the Universe." Will any of us have the time to participate? I've barely had the chance to look at the proceedings from the last three conferences.

Francesco Rossi, our engineer, is telling Rich about an upgrade to our computer network. We have a dozen computers here, running a dozen different operating systems: DEC-Unix and Linux and various versions of Windows, Macintosh. Once again, being fluent in more than one "language" is important!

Juan, a retired solar astronomer, is now our librarian; he's eager for the computer connections to be done, so that our catalog can go on line with the Vatican's back in Rome. Chris, an expert on stellar spectra, is also looking forward to using those computers for the next summer school session.

Every other year, the Observatory sponsors an intensive 4-week summer school in some aspect of astronomy. Twenty-five beginning graduate students from around the world come to learn about astronomy . . . and each other. The school is free. Our only restriction on choosing students is that they have to be the best in their field, and no more than two may come from any one country. About two-thirds of the students are from developing nations, and we subsidize their expenses. We've had seven sessions of summer schools now, 175 students; some 85 percent of them are still in astronomy, a remarkable record. Our faculty read like a Who's Who in astronomy (Vera Rubin, David Latham, George and Marsha Reicke, and Mike A'Hearn). But, then, the list of alums is beginning to read like a Who's Who, too.

My time after coffee is spent downstairs, working in the meteorite lab. The time flies. I know there's more writing I'm supposed to be doing, but that can wait until this evening. Right now, I'm just enjoying myself, pouring over my little rocks, and letting my mind roam as I try to imagine what sort of processes could have made them look the way they look today . . .

And before I know it, it's 1:30. Time for *pranzo*. My community has the big meal of the day now: a simple but delicious feast, courses of pasta, meat, salad, and fruit. The table conversation is one of the best parts of being a Jesuit. When a half dozen Ph.D.s start talking, you feel like you're getting university credits just for listening in. If learning is your passion, this is heaven.

After, we gather in the chapel for a quiet prayer. Then it's to our rooms to rest through the heat of the afternoon.

Game Theory

I wake up again around five. Soon enough, I'll be climbing the stairs back to my office to work until midnight.

But for now, I spend an hour in prayer . . . contemplating . . .

Is my life any different since I became a Jesuit? Oh, yes. None of the apartments I lived in before I entered the society were as small as my room is now . . . or as lavishly set as this palace on the hills over-looking Lake Albano. The companionship of girlfriends was very different from the community life I live now; but in none of those relationships did I really feel my gifts were so valued, or my weaknesses so accepted and cared for. The rules of obedience, from the structure of the day to this assignment at the Vatican, have put me under constraints I did not have before, but they're constraints of my choosing, which, like the rules of a sonnet, give me a framework to create a wonderfully fulfilled life.

And in the days when NASA grants were paying my bills I never had this freedom to choose what I would study, and how I would study it.

Is my science any different? No, but yes. My religion does not give me any shortcuts to the scientific truth. I cannot solve equations by infused knowledge; nor does the laying on of hands stop my hard disk from crashing! And yet, the whole experience of being a scientist is different for me now. It's not in what I do, but why I do it.

Frankly, my work in and of itself is not important. But what is important is that there are Jesuits representing the Church, representing religion, doing science. It doesn't matter who the Jesuit is; it doesn't matter what the science is. Simply that someone like me exists, a living witness to the Church's commitment to truth and the scientist's commitment to God, is what matters.

As a student I did science for the recognition—the pat on the head from my advisor, the three lines of fame in *Sky and Telescope*. When that paled, I did it just because it was the only job I knew how to do. But now . . . to be honest, now I'll never know if any recognition I get is due to my own achievements or merely my Vatican connection. But it doesn't matter. I can finally do science for just the love of knowledge, the joy of discovery, the sheer fun of it. And to throw credit on the Church and the science that I represent.

And is my religion any different? No, but yes. Popular thinking to the contrary, the mysteries of the quantum or the grandeur of the big bang aren't what give me faith. They never were. But as I see the pattern of Creation unfolding, over and over . . . complexity from the simplest of rules, beauty from the surprising interplay of basic forces . . . I begin to get a closer appreciation of the personality of the Creator.

Sometimes doing science feels like nothing so much as fiddling with a puzzle, playing a game. But I'm getting to play with the best game master of them all.

PART ONE

UPON THESE ROCKS

ALIENS AT THE VATICAN

MY FIRST reaction on arriving at the Specola Vaticana—the Vatican Observatory—was one of stunned astonishment. A thousand meteorites, all in one place. These rocks had fallen from outer space. And now they were "mine."

In many cases they'd been seen making a bright fireball through the air, and been collected near craters formed when they'd hit the ground. Others were stray bits of iron, or grayish rock, that didn't look like anything from around here. Each bore the name of the place on Earth where they'd been found. Some, like Sacramento Mountains, were metallic iron, though rich also in nickel and other metals, etched and polished to show a pattern of interlocking crystals. Some were stone: Farmington, like most of these, was made of millimeter-sized balls of rock called chondrules; other stony meteorites, like Juvinas, looked like flows of lava from some extraterrestrial volcanism. And a third group, like Eagle Station, mixed iron and stone in roughly equal proportions.

Regardless of their structure, though, their chemical compositions and elemental isotopes differed from any rock on Earth. They really were aliens from outer space. Collected over a period of some 200 years, now they sat in carefully labeled little plastic bags in drawers in a room in the Pope's summer home.

I knew why they were here. But what was I doing here?

I had joined the Jesuits at the ripe age of 37, with a career in planetary sciences safely behind me. I'd played at being a high-powered researcher at MIT and Harvard, and I turned my back on it to become a professor at a small eastern college. Deciding, finally, on entering "religious life," I had been looking forward to continuing that small-college teaching at one of the two dozen universities operated by the Jesuits across the United States. With that end in mind, for 4 years I'd studied philosophy and theology and the Jesuit way of proceeding. But a letter from Rome had changed all that.

Someone had seen my résumé, the names of the papers I had written—a long while back now. A few of those papers had been about meteorites. One, dating from 1977, had helped fuel the "are-meteorites-from-asteroids?" debate. But all my work had been theoretical. I'd never actually touched a real meteorite before.

Still, when Rome said to join the Vatican Observatory, my duty was clear. I'd taken a vow of obedience. However, personnel assignments are not quite the same as ex-cathedra pronouncements on faith and mores; they came with no guarantee that this assignment would be infallibly correct.

Arriving by train from Rome, my first view approaching Castel Gandolfo began as the little railroad car came out of a long, dark tunnel into a volcanic crater. To the left sparkled a lake, incredibly blue in the June sunlight. To the right, at the top of the crater rim, stood a 400-year-old palace, the Pope's summer residence, topped by two telescope domes. That soft beige pile of stone would be my new home.

Castel Gandolfo was built on land once part of the Imperial Palace of the Emperor Domitian (about A.D. 90). He was the first emperor to systematically persecute Christians as a matter of state policy. His palace is now the Pope's summer gardens and home.

The papal palace itself was built as a villa by Matteo Barbarini around 1590. He became Pope Urban VIII, the pope behind the trial of Galileo. His palace is now an astronomical observatory.

The building itself was incorporated into papal territory by Pope Clement XIV, who in the 1700s caused the Jesuits to be suppressed for nearly 50 years. Since the mid-1930s, one wing has served as a community for Jesuits, working at the Vatican Observatory.

I found the meteorites themselves stored in the first floor of that wing, directly under our quarters and over the barracks housing the Swiss Guards. Between the 24-hour surveillance of the Italian police and the Swiss Guards in their colorful Renaissance uniforms— designed by Michelangelo, I was told—I realized that this collection had to be probably the best-guarded set of meteorites in the world!

The meteorites had been thoroughly catalogued in the 1950s by a Jesuit, E. W. Salpeter, long since gone to his eternal reward. In the 1980s, the American meteoriticist Elbert King had joined two Italian scientists, Rosamaria Salvatori and Andriana Maras, in reinventorying the collection. But since then, the meteorites had been moved about several times. Though still labeled, and protected in plastic bags, they'd all been tossed together in a strange jumble. I didn't know much about curation, but I knew my first task would be simply to sort things out. Armed with a catalog and a large empty floor, I emptied all the drawers and started packing the samples back in, one by one, in alphabetical order.

A necessary job, and a good way to reinventory the collection, this also gave me a great way to become familiar with the look and feel of a meteorite.

When I had arrived at the Specola the director, Father George Coyne, had given me my marching orders: "Do good science." But he had left it to my own devices to decide what science to do.

I thought about all the computer models of planetary evolution I used to work on. A spacecraft on its way to Jupiter was due to arrive in a year or two; I could dust off and update my models of Jupiter's moons. Or I could write different computer models to predict the shapes and sizes of its dust rings.

For the next couple of years, I spent my time mostly on such pursuits. I also learned how to use the telescopes. I observed the impact of Shoemaker-Levy 9 into the clouds of Jupiter, and recorded the shadows of the moons of Saturn dancing across the rings during the 1995 ring-plane crossing. But mostly I played with computer models of the thermal structure of the moons of Jupiter, discovering many bugs in my computer programs along with a few scientific insights.

Yet the meteorites kept calling me.

A thousand pieces of outer space sat in those cabinets. What could they tell me about their origins? What could they tell me about the places they'd been, and the things they had seen?

Since the Apollo program in the 1960s, the chemical study of meteorites had made huge advances. It was now possible to take a microgram of stuff, hit it with a beam of electrons or ions, and take an image of incredibly tiny structures, almost to the nanometer scale. It was also possible to evaporate off individual atoms from each tiny crystal and count the different types of isotopes, seeing whether this particular rock had incorporated extra bits of supernova dust when it was formed. It was possible to count the isotopes formed by the regular decay of radioactive species, nature's internal clocks, and measure its age to ever-higher precision . . . and say with confidence that this grain must have needed 4,501,000,000 years to accumulate these radionuclide daughter isotopes, and it was indeed younger than the neighbor grain that had collected a few more daughter isotopes into its crystal structure over 4,502,000,000 years.

But all that work took equipment: fancy, expensive, and difficult to maintain equipment. We had neither the budget nor the staff to set up a radioisotope lab or bring in a scanning electron microscope.

And besides, someone else was already doing that work, and doing it with years more experience than I could bring to the task. What I wanted to do was something new. I just couldn't see what. Clearly, it was time to go back to the rocks to ask if they had any ideas.

I looked over the collection again. It had been put together by a nineteenth-century French nobleman, the Marquis de Mauroy. Since his death, the collection had only been expanded by the occasional donation or trade. The Marquis himself had gotten his samples the good old-fashioned way: buying them from dealers. People like our Marquis had kept the real meteorite collectors, like Charles Olivier and Oscar Monnig, in business through the late 1800s as they went around the world buying up meteorites from local farmers and ranchers. As a result, his collection—our collection—had little pieces of lots of different meteorites; but very few big pieces, few "main masses" with stuff to spare. Destructive experiments were out.

The age of this collection posed a second problem. Most of the samples, even those that had been collected immediately after they were seen to fall, were now more than a hundred years old. Rocks from Earth itself come from an environment that is more or less in equilibrium with our wet, oxygen-rich atmosphere; but meteorites do not. They're full of stuff like tiny flecks of metallic iron that will start to rust away in no time, just sitting on a museum shelf. How would my measurements—whatever measurements they might be—be affected by this chemical change? I scratched my head over that one a long time, then finally came to the only possible solution . . . I decided not to worry about it just yet.

Looking at the rocks, I thought back to my computer models. You never understand a process in nature until you can write a computer model to simulate it. That's not because the computer model itself tells you anything you'd particularly believe; I knew to trust my output only so far. But the process of constructing the model in the first place meant writing down all the relevant equations; that meant you had to know what the relevant equations were.

And it meant having numbers to shove into those equations. That meant getting a handle on reasonable values for each of the variables that you thought was important in the process you were modeling. Collecting those equations and those values, and then finding out which ones were the ones that really mattered, was the heart of the work.

One of the numbers I was using all the time was "density." Just like you can guess what's in your birthday present by picking it up and feeling its heft, you can guess the inside of a planet by noting its *density*—the total mass divided by the total volume. Ice has a density of about one gram per cubic centimeter (g/cm³), rock is roughly three, and iron around eight. So you measure the density of a planet, and then mix and match among those components.

But... "About?" "Roughly?" "Around?" We should be able to do better than that.

I remembered how hard it had been to find density numbers for ordinary Earth rocks. And for meteorites, finding those values was virtually impossible. Density... such an obvious quantity, presumably easy to measure. Why were meteorite density values so rare?

Density is mass divided by volume. Well, mass was easy enough... just put the sample on a scale. I looked around the Observatory, and came across a beautiful two-pan balance with weights accurate to a hundredth of a gram, enclosed in a glass-and-mahogany case; the kind of quality you just don't see any more. Indeed, on the top of the case a plaque identified the scale as a gift of the manufacturer, an Austrian scientific company, to His Holiness Pope Pius XI. That put this scale's vintage at around 1930. But it still functioned. And I was just barely old enough to remember being taught how to use such a scale. (Students have everything digital nowadays.)

Mass is easy. But what about volume? How does one find a volume of something as irregular as a meteorite... without carving it into a perfect cube at least? Well, a mere 2500 years ago in the Greek colony of Syracuse on what's now Sicily (nowadays just an hour's plane ride south of Castel Gandolfo), Archimedes had worked that one out. You remember the story. Pondering how to measure the volume of the king's crown, he watched the level of his bath water rise as his slaves lowered him into the tub and, inspired, ran stark naked down the streets of Syracuse shouting "Eureka."

Modern scientists run a slight variation on this technique. You tie a string to the rock, weigh it by dangling it from a scale, and then see how the weight changes when the rock is dangled into water. But ultimately it's the same principle.

The only trouble was, my meteorites were rusting away just sitting in the Roman humidity. No way was I going to actually immerse them into water.

Later, when I was at our observatory in Arizona, I told my colleague Dan Britt what I was trying to do. He pointed out a different problem with the Archimedean method.

"Contamination? Real geologists have solved that problem years ago," he explained. Unlike me, he considered himself a real geologist. "You use a device called a 'pycnometer.' Instead of water, it uses helium gas. Helium is completely inert, so there's no contamination."

He explained how it worked. The rock is sealed in a chamber of known volume and flushed with helium at room pressure. A second chamber of known volume with helium at, say, two atmospheres pressure, is attached to the first chamber. Open the valve between them and see what the final pressure turns out to be. The bigger the rock, the more space it takes up in its chamber, the less room there is for helium, and so the higher the final pressure. Collect the data on a computer and it'll correct for temperature and other effects, and read out the volume of the sample. "In fact," Dan told me, "a guy named Mike Geddis over at the Geology Department built one of these devices for his thesis; it's just the right size for your meteorites."

"Great!" I said. "Let's ship it to Italy and get to work."

"Not so fast," he warned me. "There's one major problem." I waited for him to explain. "Now ask yourself, why are we interested in measuring meteorite density?"

"Models of—" I started.

"Asteroids!" he proclaimed, nodding, not waiting for me to finish. "Exactly!"

To be honest, I hadn't thought of making models of asteroids. But I decided to hear him out.

"We're finally sending spacecraft past asteroids and measuring their densities. We have numbers for the little Mars moons, Phobos and Deimos, which most of us think are captured asteroids. And the Galileo spacecraft got a density for asteroid Ida while passing through the asteroid belt on its way to Jupiter. Next year they're going to launch the NEAR spacecraft to go past asteroid Mathilde and on to asteroid Eros. Something called Deep Space One is going to go past an asteroid, too . . . there are all sorts of these missions being planned.

But what good is an asteroid density if you don't have any meteorite densities to compare them against?"

"Wait a minute," I interrupted. "The guys who measured Ida's density compared it to different meteorites. As I recall, they said its density proved the asteroid was similar to an ordinary chondrite, and ruled out a composition like stony-iron meteorites. Their paper quoted meteorite densities for ordinary chondrites, and for stony-irons."

"Funny thing about that," Dan replied. "I looked it up. The stony-iron numbers aren't there."

I looked at Dan, stunned. "Not there?"

"Check out the reference they cited. The numbers they quoted for stony-irons aren't in that reference. Or anywhere else, as far as I can tell."

"They made up those numbers?" I asked. He said nothing. "But those guys are big-name, reputable scientists. And the numbers they quoted sounded quite reasonable."

"Sure, they sounded reasonable. That's how they got away with it. Actually, they probably just inserted a reasonable sounding number when they were writing the first draft and never got around to checking it out. I don't think they were being deliberately dishonest, just sloppy. But the fact is, they couldn't quote real numbers because, for stony-irons at least, there are no real numbers in the literature to quote. I know. I spent a month combing the journals for reported values of meteorite densities and porosities."

"So, we've got some stony-irons in the Vatican collection. Let's go measure them."

"No, you missed the point. That's still comparing apples and oranges. You're neglecting something called porosity."

He pushed some papers off his desk and drew me a sketch. "Look here. The volume that a pycnometer measures is the volume of just the grains of rock itself, right? The helium can get into all the cracks and voids and pore spaces. Helium has the tiniest molecules in nature; it can get through anything. But the volumes of the asteroids that these guys used were just based on images taken from hundreds of kilometers away. Their volume includes everything, from the tiniest voids in the rock to caves and fissures big enough to hide a Buick."

"Yeah," I answered. "But how much space can that really be?"

"Sand on a beach is 50 percent empty space," he told me. "Typical sandstone, like the rocks that line the Grand Canyon, can be 30 percent pore space, easily. The point is, we don't know. I've searched the literature for porosity measurements of meteorites, and they're darn hard to find. One of the most common classes of meteorites, LL chondrites, has had only two porosities published. One was 3 percent, the other was 30 percent. Which are we supposed to believe?"

"So if the helium gizmo gives us the wrong kind of density, how do you measure a porosity?"

"Actually, you need the helium pycnometer for the grain volume. But then you have to find another way to measure a bulk volume. The relative difference between those two volumes tells you the volume of the pore spaces—the porosity."

So all we had to do was figure out a way of measuring the outside volume of the rock. We thought up all sorts of schemes, and read about other people's attempts.

In the past, many workers had just dipped the rocks into water, ignoring the contamination problem, and hoping that water's surface tension would keep it from penetrating the smaller cracks. (But there was no way to be sure just how valid that assumption was.)

I thought of wrapping the meteorites in plastic; before trying it out on one of my rocks, however, I first tried to wrap tightly a pile of sugar cubes. After dunking them in water, more often than not they came out soggy.

The Japanese had actually carved some of their meteorites into perfect cubes. No way I was going to cut up all my samples, however. Besides, who knew how much internal cracking was caused by the cutting process?

The answer came over a cup of cappuccino, back in Italy, in our kitchen in Castel Gandolfo. In America I never put sugar in my coffee, but the strong bitter Italian brew combines with their coarse-grained sugar perfectly. (The same sugar is lousy for making chocolate chip cookies, however.) Pouring a spoonful of the sweet stuff into my *spuma,* watching it dribble off my spoon like a fluid, made me start to think . . .

Take a cup of known volume, fill it with sugar, and weigh it. That tells you the density of the sugar. Take the same cup, stick the rock in the bottom, and fill the rest with sugar. Weigh it again. Somehow, the difference between the two weights should be telling you something about the density of the rock compared to the density of the sugar, right? A page of algebra later, I came up with a relatively simple formula. It should work. And when you're done, all you have to do is brush off the sugar.

I tried it out on a series of ordinary chondrites; it seemed to work. Dan Britt latched onto the idea immediately, and went about improving it. Instead of plastic cups, he got some flat-topped beakers. Instead of my 1930s scales (which, while elegant, took forever to use) he found me a triple-beam balance. He bought a vibrating platform from a dentist supply house to shake down the powder in a repeatable fashion. And best of all, he replaced my angular, irregularly packing sugar with 40-micrometer (μm) glass beads. "I have this friend in the University optical shop," he explained. "They get these beads by the barrelful to use for glass polishing."

In April, Dan and his family stayed with us for a month in Castel Gandolfo, getting the lab set up. From then through June I kept at it, measuring about a hundred different samples from the Vatican collection. We presented our results at meetings in Berlin and Hawaii. Finally, we wrote them up and submitted them for publication in the journal *Meteoritics and Planetary Sciences.* After a few suggested improvements from the referees, the paper was accepted and published. Our technique, and our measurements, are now part of the scientific literature.

What's more, our bulk density measurements showed that meteorites were systematically 10 or 20 percent more dense than the asteroids we thought they'd come from . . . even taking their porosity into account.

How could that be? We know meteorites come from the asteroid belt; we've actually traced the orbits of a few of them while they were streaking through the air, and all of them go back to the asteroid belt. Besides, the detailed colors of meteorites—their spectra—show the same mineralogical features as the spectra of asteroids. Asteroids must be made up of meteorite-type material. So how could they be 20 percent less dense? Are they hollow?

Well . . . maybe. Not hollow like a cheap chocolate Easter-egg, but full of void spaces, like the gaps between the candies in a pile of jelly beans. Asteroids are not solid rocks; they're piles of rubble! And loose piles of rubble, at that.

So what? Well . . .

Soldiers in the Civil War discovered that forts made of solid rock would shatter when hit by cannon balls, but fort walls made of sand and wood could absorb a month of cannoning without giving an inch. Asteroids should react the same way. Sending Bruce Willis out to blow up a rogue asteroid would be a whole lot tougher job than Hollywood had portrayed.

On the other hand, a mining expedition that goes out to collect valuable minerals from the asteroids may not need to bring any dynamite . . . just a shovel and bucket. It all depends on how big the pieces are, which is something we really don't know yet.

But it was no surprise when NEAR finally did encounter Mathilde and discovered that its density, too, was way lower than previously expected . . . and that judging from the many huge craters on its surface, it had endured numerous massive collisions with other bits of space debris, without flying apart.

But our work didn't stop there. Once I had a pile of data points, densities, and porosities, I did what all deep-thinking scientists do. I plotted every variable against every other possible variable, in the hope that maybe some pattern might jump out at me.

And one did.

Plot the porosity we measured against the bulk density, and it becomes evident for the ordinary chondrites that the data points tend to fall into three groups, dividing itself pretty cleanly into the well-known chemical groups of low, medium, and high iron content. What's more, these three groups fell on more or less straight lines sloping downward to the right, so that the lowest density samples of each group had the highest porosity, while high-density rocks had low porosity.

Well, what did you expect? Take a rock of a known composition and add pore space, and, of course, the density will drop. What's so profound about that? In fact, the density will obviously drop to zero when the porosity is 100 percent, whereas if the porosity is zero, then the bulk density must be equal to the grain density. These "lines" were just telling me that all high-iron chondrites should have about the same grain density; all medium-iron samples a slightly lower grain density; and so on. But I should have known that, too. After all, meteorites of each group are made up of the same minerals—that's how they got to be grouped together into low- and medium- and high-iron populations in the first place.

Ought to have the same grain density . . . but they don't, actually. While there is a roughly linear trend, there are also a whole bunch of meteorites in each group that lie way off that trend. How come?

Time to plot some more data. Some meteorites were seen to *fall*. Others were just stumbled across by some farmer, who would only *find* them after they had been sitting on the warm, moist ground for who knows how long. The porosity of the "fall" meteorites could range anywhere from a few percent up to, in some extreme cases, 20 percent or more. The porosity of almost all the "find" meteorites was zero. Zilch. No pore space in those guys. And those were precisely the guys who lay farthest off the line.

Nothing deep and profound about that, either. When meteorites rust, it's because water gets into them—through those pore spaces—and reaches flecks of iron that turn into iron oxide . . . which then fills up the pore spaces. So naturally meteorites that had been left out in the weather would have very little pore space left. It's all been choked with rust.

I had been worried, in the back of my mind, about using our hundred-year-old samples for just that reason. So could I say anything about how this "weathering" might have skewed our results?

Well, the density of rust is a whole lot lower than the density of iron. So by turning iron into rust, the grain densities of weathered meteorites will have dropped compared to whatever grain density they started with. Of course, for the ordinary chondrites, I could calculate what that pristine original grain density should have been, since presumably all meteorites of a given mineralogical class should have started with the same grain density, which you could get off those graphs, where the different classes lined up according to density and porosity. Just look up the highest grain density, of the most pristine sample, and any deviation from that density should be a measure of how weathered the meteorite had become. I had discovered a way to estimate degree of weathering.

OK. What about the bulk density? Obviously, filling up internal pores would not change the overall outside shape of the meteorite, so the bulk volume would be unchanged. Turning iron into rust means taking iron that's already in the rock, and reacting it with Earth air; as they added terrestrial oxygen, the rocks would become a little bit more massive. But compared to iron, the mass of oxygen is negligible. A fast calculation convinced me that the net growth in mass would be only a couple of percent.

Same volume? Roughly the same mass? Funny . . . that means that weathering really shouldn't change the bulk density all that much. So the bulk density now is about the same as it was when it was still out in space.

But I could guess the grain density out in space, just by looking at what mineral class the meteorite belonged to. Which meant, I had enough information to calculate a model "pristine" unweathered porosity for any ordinary chondrite. All I needed to know was what class it belonged to and what its bulk density was.

And finding bulk densities was a snap. No need for complicated helium equipment . . . a beaker, a scale, and a pile of glass beads would suffice. I started measuring bulk densities of every ordinary chondrite I could find.

Then I made one final plot. Of all my meteorites, how many had a porosity of one percent? Two percent? Three percent? And so forth. I plotted up a "histogram" that showed the real, measured porosities ranged all over the place, from zero into the teens before they finally trailed off, leaving a few samples in the 20 percent porosity range.

But when I made the same plot using my pristine porosities, almost all the meteorites had porosities clustering around 10 percent! This was telling me something profound. I only wished I knew what.

One chilly February morning, some 2 years after we'd started this work, I was visiting my old friend from graduate school days, Cliff

Stoll, who now lived and worked in the Bay Area. We were riding a BART train from San Francisco back to his home in Oakland, having spent that Saturday morning attending a live radio show, *West Coast Live*. (It's hosted by an old friend of Cliff's, Sedge Thompson.) We'd talked about the show and the weather and the coffee and bagels we'd consumed. And somewhere under the bay, I started telling Cliff about my latest research.

". . . 10 percent!" I ended with a dramatic flourish. "But what does it mean?"

"Guy," asked Cliff. "Why are there meteorites?"

"I . . . huh? What are you talking about?"

"I mean, we think that the planets formed out of gas and dust in a proto-solar nebula, right?" I nodded. "And the meteorites are the remnants of that original cloud of gas and dust," he continued. Again, that's the standard story we'd learned in graduate school. "Then why are they rocks?"

"I don't get it," I answered. "What do you mean? Of course they're rocks."

"But if they started out as dust in a gas, why aren't all the meteorites today still just interplanetary dust bunnies?"

Damn. I'd never thought about that before. What squeezed the meteorites into rocks? "Well . . . maybe they got compressed by gravity when they were accreted into bigger asteroids."

Cliff gave me a scornful look. "What asteroid is big enough to have the gravity to do that job? You said yourself that even sandstones on Earth have a porosity of 30 percent. But what asteroid has the pressure in its center as high as you get just a few kilometers deep into the Earth's crust? Yet your meteorites have a porosity of only 10 percent. So something must have packed them, and packed them pretty tight. What was it?"

I paused some more to think. "Impacts? All the things that make craters out there . . ."

"And then what blows the asteroids into rubble piles, and knocks bits of meteorite off the asteroids and onto Earth-crossing orbits?"

"Impacts . . . all the things that make craters out there."

"So the same impacts that fluff up asteroids also compress them into rocks?" He gave me a real scornful look then. "Maybe. But I'm not so sure. How does a dust bunny transmit the shock wave of an impact? By definition a hypervelocity impact happens too fast to transfer momentum smoothly, and it's the change in momentum that is the force term in the force-per-area quantity we call compression. Of course, maybe you had different episodes of accretion and impaction, but then you have to worry about how brecciation occurs . . ."

We kept arguing about the details of impact mechanics and the structure of the meteorite fabric . . . and suddenly, I realized that my porosity data were giving me a window into a whole suite of events going on in the early solar system. My numbers were fundamental constraints on the physical processes that these rocks had seen. And hadn't seen. They were numbers that were forcing me to ask a question I'd never considered before. Exactly why were there meteorites?

I remember as a kid learning about the "scientific method." A scientist, I was told, sees a problem, creates a hypothesis, and tests it with experiments. But I'd done just the opposite.

I had performed a bunch of experiments. They had led me to a hypothesis. That hypothesis challenged me with a question I had never thought of before.

One thousand aliens sat in little plastic bags in a dusty room at the Vatican. They'd come to Earth to talk to me. But when they spoke, it was not to preach answers, but to raise questions.

THE CASE OF THE FIERY FINGERS

In all the Earth there is probably no mental occupation quite as fascinating as that of finding clues and then accounting for them, which is all that detective work really is and about all that astronomy really is.

—*Erle Stanley Gardner,* The Case of the Fiery Fingers

O ROCKS really fall out of the sky? Following the report around 1800 of a meteorite fall in New England, President Thomas Jefferson is reputed to have said, "It is easier to believe that two Yankee professors would lie than that stones would fall from heaven." At least, that's the story, though no one has been able to prove Jefferson actually said it.

But in his book *Cosmic Debris: Meteorites in History,* John G. Burke actually documents an even more startling quote. In 1803, after Jean-Baptiste Biot of the French Academy of Sciences investigated a fall of stones near L'Aigle and reported that they did indeed appear to be masses foreign to our planet, Jefferson wrote to the American naturalist Andrew Elliot, saying:

> The exuberant imagination of a Frenchman . . . runs away with his judgment. It even creates facts for him which never happened, and

he tells them with good faith . . . The evidence of nature, derived from experience, must be put into one scale, and in the other the testimony of man, his ignorance, the deception of his senses, his lying disposition.

But contrary to Thomas Jefferson's scorn, meteorites are indeed rocks fallen from the sky. When a rock sitting by itself on the ground is completely different from any of the normal rocks in the area; when it has a physical and chemical structure different from any Earth rock; when it has isotope abundances not seen on Earth (outside of a nuclear reactor); when it is covered with a thin black sheet of molten rock, as if it had been heated strongly while flying through the air at an enormous rate; then it is likely that the rock is something from not around here.

More than 15,000 samples of such rocks are known. Of them, nearly a thousand have actually been observed to fall out of the sky. Of those, only four have been photographed while falling with enough evidence to calculate their orbits before they hit the Earth; still, those four all have orbits that trace back to the belt of asteroids between Jupiter and Mars. But beyond these few clues, we have no direct evidence for where these meteorites come from. It's a mystery.

Some meteorites are basaltic. That is to say, they have a mineralogy and texture very much like that of rocks derived from the lava of volcanoes on Earth. The mineralogy is quite distinctive. Of the roughly 70 basaltic meteorites known in the mid-1970s, 33 of them were of a type called *eucrites* (the Greek means well-formed crystals), which are plagioclase-pyroxene meteorites; another 9 were *diogenites,* which are pure pyroxene; and 21 of the basaltic meteorites were *howardites,* which appear to be a mechanical mixture of eucrite and diogenite crystals. These three types account for 90 percent of all known basaltic meteorites. In addition, stony-iron meteorites of a type called *mesosiderites* appear to be mixtures of iron and howardite material; back in the 1970s, there were 28 known samples of this type of meteorite. The statistics, as we shall see, are important.

Basaltic meteorites offer us important clues about meteorite origins because we think we understand the formation of terrestrial basalts pretty well. We can observe volcanic eruptions, and watch the fiery fingers of lava poke out through fissures in the Earth and claw their way down a mountainside, then cool to form new rock. And we can use different geochemical techniques to infer the kind of rock that must have melted to form them.

Thus, with basaltic meteorites we ought to be able to look back, through the time when they were melted, to see what the conditions must have been like in the primitive asteroid before the melting took place. If we could model these conditions, we might be able to identify the source of the meteorites.

We know how long ago these basalts were formed from the abundances of radioactive isotopes in the samples: the isotopes tell us that the melting event that made this lava apparently took place 4.6 billion years ago. That's as old as the solar system itself. There's no evidence that any other geochemical alteration took place between the formation of the asteroid and the present day, except for this melting event itself. Thus, the source region of the basaltic meteorites that we deduce in our "looking back" process may represent a sample of what primitive material in the solar system looked like just after the planets were formed, before they started their geochemical and geophysical evolution into the places we see today.

Basalts consist of a small number of well-defined minerals. Each mineral has a distinct crystal structure, made of a few specific elements: silicon, oxygen, magnesium, iron, aluminum, and calcium. The chemical bonding properties of these six elements control the shape of the crystal. Any other element that wants to find a place in the crystal must squeeze itself into a site normally occupied by one of these six elements.

Of special interest in basaltic rocks are the trace elements known as rare earth elements (REE). By noting the small differences in relative abundances from the lightest to the heaviest REE, we can pick up clues about the chemical changes that these elements have undergone . . . in particular, the affinity of crystals for the REE in the source region where the basalts were made. After all, not every mineral in the source region will melt itself into the lava; the REE tell us about minerals present in the source region that otherwise did not participate in the melting. Two origin scenarios are possible for basaltic lava.

In the first scenario, we start with a source region consisting of several different solid minerals. We partially melt this region; some of those minerals melt into the lava, others may not. Then, before the rest of the source region can be completely melted, the first bits of lava formed are quickly erupted onto the surface of the planet, where it is flash-frozen. The result is a dark rock with very tiny crystals, whose composition matches the composition of the partial melt made below the surface of the planet.

Such a scenario requires a rapid release of lava; examples of such lava flooding are the mare regions of the Moon and the lavas erupting from the volcanoes in Hawaii. Lava frozen in this way often looks like a "sponge" because it is full of holes (called "vesicles") which are produced by gas bubbles frozen into the lava as it cools.

However, there's a second scenario to consider. We know that most volcanoes on Earth store their lava in a subterranean region called a magma chamber before erupting it onto the surface. Within this chamber, molten lava is slowly cooling off; as heat is lost, crystals of certain minerals begin to form within the chamber.

This slow cooling means that the crystal growth is relatively slow. This gives the crystals time to grow to a relatively large [1- to 10-millimeter (mm)] size. These crystals themselves make a distinctive-looking rock, with a distinctive crystal texture; but the major minerals in the rock, which depend only on its major element abundances, may not be all that different from the bulk original lava—or from the rock formed by our first scenario.

Furthermore, after most of the magma has refrozen and crystallized, the last bits of melted lava could be suddenly erupted onto the surface and flash-frozen. That would produce a rock indistinguishable from the first scenario as far as its mineralogy, crystal size, presence of vesicles, and other physical traits are concerned.

Thus, given just a small piece of a meteorite sample today, the mystery remains: which of these scenarios best describes the process that formed this meteorite? And by inference, which best describes the original chemical and physical state of the planet where these meteorites came from in the first place?

This question can be answered by looking at the trace elements in the minerals, in particular the rare earth elements. Although the major minerals may be the same in all the rocks formed by any of the scenarios described here, each scenario will form a rock that has a distinctly different abundance pattern of rare earth elements.

To model the evolution of REE abundances, we need several ideas, and a certain amount of data.

In order to start a specific computation, we must have some idea of the original rare earth element abundances in the source region from which the lava came and a good quantitative starting guess for the original mineral composition of the source region.

We must have a general idea of which sort of process produced the basalt in question: Which scenario are we going to model? Does our rock sample represent lava that was a partial melt of a source region deep inside the planet, or was it a partial crystallization of a totally molten lava chamber, or the residual melt from such a partially crystallized chamber?

Given a process, we need to know a specific description of what other minerals could have been present, unmelted, in chemical equilibrium with the lava from which our sample came; and the pressure and temperature in the magma chamber. Those hidden minerals and the pressure and temperature conditions all affect how the REE behave.

To complete the model, we need to know (or solve for) a numerical value for the fraction of the source lava that was melted or crystallized at the moment the composition of our rock was set.

And, obviously, we also need to know the abundances of the rare earth elements in the meteorite samples today. It is against these data that the model is tested. If our model does not predict the trace element abundances actually observed, then we haven't solved the puzzle.

In the early 1960s, neutron activation analysis—a technique requiring a nuclear reactor to irradiate the samples—was finally precise enough to measure abundances of such rare elements. Like most elemental abundances, the abundances of the REE vary by factors of

10 from element to element. However, a trick for comparing these abundances from rock to rock had been developed: in every sample, the raw number abundance of each element is divided by the standard abundance seen in primitive carbon-bearing meteorites, thought to represent the primordial abundances of these elements in the solar system. This ratio to "cosmic abundances" then presumably shows how much our sample has been changed from whatever abundance was originally present when the primitive asteroid that is the source of the meteorite was formed.

In the early 1970s, a young professor at MIT, John Lewis, proposed a grand model for the origin of solar system chemistry. Lewis had been a student of Harold Urey's at University of California, San Diego; Urey, a Nobel Prize winner for his discovery of isotopes, had been interested since the late 1940s in trying to explain the chemical composition of the planets. Lewis used a computer—at that time, an exotic tool for a chemist—to predict numerically which minerals would be in chemical equilibrium with a gas of solar composition at the various pressures and temperatures predicted for the theorized gas nebula surrounding the early Sun.

Lewis went on to show how this one theory, known as the equilibrium condensation theory, could explain the densities of the terrestrial planets, the compositions of the clouds of Jupiter, and the densities and surface features of the outer solar system moons. His work inspired a small army of graduate students, to extend this line of research into the way planets were physically formed, how atmospheres evolved on those planets, and even how interstellar grains of exotic composition could be made around other stars.

A colleague of Lewis at MIT, Thomas McCord, was an observational astronomer who had developed a technique for taking and interpreting reflectance spectra of solar system objects. He would use a telescope to collect light reflected off a solar system object, pass that light through each of two dozen different-colored filters, and precisely measure the intensity of each color with an electronic phototube. Then he could compare these colors with the spectra of laboratory samples to try to guess what samples best matched the colors seen at the telescope.

McCord's primary work was on mapping the mineralogy of the Moon. By observing various lunar regions and comparing the different Moon spectra with spectra of samples returned by the Apollo mission, he could connect up the parts of the Moon we had visited with the much vaster regions that Apollo never got to.

With the wind-down of the Apollo program in the early 1970s, he turned his technique to other bodies and began taking spectra of various asteroids.

A student of his, Michael Gaffey, took spectra of meteorite samples in the laboratory and compared these spectra with the asteroids. One of the first results of this work was to show that the bright asteroid Vesta (the brighter the asteroid, the easier it is to take a spectrum) has a reflectance that looked in great detail like the reflectance spectrum of basaltic meteorites. No other asteroid came close to matching this spectrum. Vesta was unique.

Meanwhile, at the University of Oregon, a young graduate student from Britain named Michael Drake was completing his doctoral dissertation work on the behavior of trace elements in geophysical systems. Certain basalts contain both large, well-formed crystals of a given mineral and an amorphous or fine-grained mass that formed by the rapid freezing of the lava from which those minerals crystallized. By measuring the abundance of a given REE in both crystal and frozen melt, one could determine the natural ratio, called the *partition coefficient,* representing quantitatively the degree to which that particular element would distribute itself between melt and mineral.

With a numerical value in hand for how much a given REE is likely to go into a given mineral, it becomes possible to model numerically how much of that REE is expected to be found in a melt of a given composition from a source region of a given composition. Previous work had looked at the partition coefficients for most REE and most major minerals; Drake's thesis involved the last of partition coefficient measurements, involving the element europium whose partition coefficient was a delicate function of temperature and oxygen abundance. Once this experimental work was complete, detailed modeling of basaltic systems could begin.

Ed Stolper, a senior at Harvard in 1975, as part of his undergraduate thesis, proposed the partial melt model for eucrites, based on major element ratios (in particular the iron/magnesium ratio seen in the basalt). The same iron/magnesium ratio could be produced by the other processes, but it would involve assuming very high iron contents which seemed unreasonable in light of the iron/magnesium ratios seen in Moon rocks and other meteorites; Stolper's model assumed iron/magnesium ratios that were in line with the other samples.

His model also suggested a way in which the diogenites and howardites could be tied in with the eucrites. His experiments on minerals synthesized in the lab suggested that a source region rich in plagioclase, pyroxene, olivine, and metallic iron (in uncertain proportions) would partially melt to form a lava of plagioclase and pyroxene, similar to the eucrites. If the abundance of pyroxene were greater than the abundance of plagioclase, continued melting after all the plagioclase had melted and the eucrite lava was expelled from the system would produce diogenitelike pyroxene lava. After this lava was erupted onto the surface of the asteroid, repeated impacts by meteoroids would break up and mix these rocks into howardites, in a fashion similar to the way that lunar breccia rocks (returned by the Apollo program) appeared to have been formed.

From 1971 to 1975 I was a student of John Lewis at MIT, finishing up my master's thesis in 1975. During that time I also took a course in observational astronomy from McCord, conducted in part by his graduate student, Mike Gaffey. Thus, the work of both Lewis' and McCord's groups was very familiar to me.

I arrived at Arizona in May 1975, to begin a Ph.D. program under the direction of Mike Drake. I spent that summer learning the mathematics of REE modeling and programming a small computer to perform these models. Our interest at the time was to model in detail the evolution of lunar basalts, especially the basalts returned by Apollo 17 in December 1972. This work was essentially complete by the spring of 1976. At that point, Drake suggested that we apply our techniques to the eucrite meteorites.

Recall the items needed to construct a numerical model for the evolution of REE abundances. They included a model for the formation of the eucrite minerals; we used Stolper's model. We needed knowledge of partition coefficients; Mike Drake's work provided those. We needed to know the observed REE patterns to test our model; those we obtained from the literature, some 10 to 15 years old at that point.

In addition, however, we needed to guess: (1) a starting mineral composition for the source region, (2) a starting REE abundance in the source region, and (3) the degree of melting of this starting composition. Given any two of these items, our model could predict the value of the third. (Of course, the model could also show that some starting conditions, or REE abundances, could be ruled out as impossible under any conditions.) The general way to solve this problem would be to show the range of possible starting conditions, REE initial abundances, and degrees of melting that would be consistent with Stolper's model for the origin of the eucrites. Such a model would not be unique, but might show an interesting range of possibilities. The fact that any model could work at all would be seen as support for Stolper's hypothesis.

However, as someone raised in Lewis' view of the solar system, I took a slightly different tack. I assumed that the primitive asteroid from which the eucrites evolved had a composition consistent with John Lewis' equilibrium condensation model. By using cosmic abundances and reasonable assumptions for what minerals ought to be present, based on his model, I calculated that the source region of the eucrite parent body ought to be roughly 5 percent plagioclase, 15 percent pyroxene, and 80 percent olivine and metallic nickel-iron. Given this starting mineralogy, and assuming initial REE abundances to be the same as cosmic abundances, I found that the REE abundances in most eucrites could be matched by a very reasonable amount of melting, 5 to 10 percent of the total source region.

Thus, we showed that Stolper's model was consistent with REE patterns seen in these meteorites; further, we showed that Lewis' model was consistent with a possible starting mineralogy for the parent body. Note that the demonstration was only at the "consistent with" level. This is better than the "not inconsistent with" level that much of planetary science has to operate under (often, the best we can do is show that a given model is "not disproved" by the facts) but no claim on uniqueness could be made.

Pleased with this result, Mike Drake and I prepared a 10-minute talk for me to give at the annual meeting of the Meteoritical Society in October 1976. Immediately before my talk, another group of scientists, from the University of Oregon (Mike Drake's old school), presented a very similar piece of work. They, however, did not use the Lewis model to guess at the starting conditions; instead, they merely followed the general procedure of showing a family of possible solutions (of which the Lewis model, which they did not recognize, was but one solution among many): a far more complex result to present than ours. In addition, their presentation was given by a graduate student from overseas whose first language was not English. As a result, their paper got much less attention than ours did.

My presentation seemed to go over pretty well. I think it helped having the other group talk first, since they made the audience aware of the general problem and the idea of using a computer model of REE element evolution to solve it.

After my presentation, Cal Tech professor Gerry Wasserburg approached me in the hallway. Not only was he one of the greats in the field, he spoke with an intimidating, drill-sergeant abruptness. I braced myself for his comments.

"That was a pretty good paper," he said. I was surprised, if relieved. He wasn't finished yet, however. "So, tell me," he continued. "Do you really believe it?"

I stopped for a moment, surprised by the question.

"Well . . . yes," I said.

"Why?" he challenged me.

"Because I think it all holds together so well. All the little details, like the compositions of the plagioclases, and trends in other trace elements, are all consistent with this picture."

His skepticism was not unexpected. Our model assumed a linear fit between abundance (relative to cosmic) and mass of the individual REE: if one element were 2 percent less abundant than the element to the right, the next element on the left should be 4 percent less abundant, as so on. In fact, the data were not so perfect; nor, indeed, were our values for the partition coefficients all that precise. (They are probably good to a factor of 2, but no better.) On the other hand, the beauty of using 15 similarly behaving REE instead of one or two other trace elements is that random error in partition coefficients or measured abundances should tend to average out when one looks not at any individual numbers but at the trend of all of them together. There are sophisticated statistical ways of fitting trends to data like ours, but, in fact, all we tried to do was to show that our model results could, by eye, be seen to be reasonably close to the measured abundances. Again, we did not pretend to present a rigorous proof, but rather an argument of strong reasonability.

My conversation with Dr. Wasserburg continued. "If all these basaltic meteorites represent the 5 percent or 10 percent of the asteroid that melted, where's the rest of the asteroid?" he asked. "Shouldn't we see nine olivine and metal rich meteorites for every eucrite?"

"No," I replied without even thinking. "You don't expect that at all, because the eucrites come from Vesta, and Vesta is still out there. We only see stuff that's been chipped off its crust. Its mantle and core, the olivine and metal, are still intact."

On reflection, however, the implication of this thought was stunning.

We had demonstrated that the eucrites could have come from a moderately sized asteroid made of ordinary minerals in cosmic proportions, which underwent a small degree of melting. That means that 90 percent of that asteroid is still in space. Either the asteroid is broken up completely, in which case we'd expect to see a large number of iron and olivine meteorites, or else it is still out there. If it is still out there, it ought to have a surface that looks like eucrites.

We could then set up a simple syllogism:

1. All eucrites come from an asteroidal parent body that is still intact and looks like basaltic achondrite material.
2. Vesta is the only asteroid in existence today that is intact and looks like basaltic achondrite material.
3. Therefore, all eucrites come from Vesta.

We had solved a problem that we didn't realize we would be able to solve. We had gone beyond the orbit determinations that tell us that meteorites come from the asteroid belt to finger the asteroid Vesta as the source of our meteorites. And we demonstrated that asteroids (or, at least, this particular asteroid) have a composition consistent with the Lewis equilibrium condensation theory.

The Consolmagno and Drake paper ("Composition and Evolution of the Eucrite Parent Body: Evidence from Rare Earth Elements," published in 1977 in the journal *Geochimica et Cosmochimica Acta*) gained acceptance over rival theories because of four factors.

The clearness of the presentation at the Meteoritical Society meeting in 1976 served as an important advertisement for the work. I owed this to Mike Drake's coaching and to the Jesuit, Father Pilot, who taught me speech back in high school—maybe the most important course I took for my scientific career.

The simplicity of the logic and the wide-ranging application of different theories allowed this small bit of work to fit in and combine many divergent pet theories. To put it another way, the emotional or intuitive feeling resulting from the paper was that "it's so neat, it ought to be true."

The theory was the first REE model of the eucrites in print in a widely read and prestigious journal, and the paper was relatively well written (thanks here to my high school English teachers) and well illustrated.

Finally, all the right political connections were made without the paper coming down on any side of a controversial political squabble. The east coast planetary scientists (Harvard and MIT) each saw a pet theory of their group used and vindicated. The southern California group saw their 15-year-old data used to good purpose. The Houston group saw lunar science techniques being applied to other solar system bodies, vindicating their claim that the money spent on lunar science would have a positive "ripple effect" on the field. Even the Oregon group was not disappointed, since one of their own—Mike Drake—was on the paper that rivaled theirs. They never challenged the methodology of our paper, or pointed out (what was true) that their methodology was in many ways more rigorous and less dependent on other theories and other models.

The paper has held up remarkably well over time. More than 20 years later, it is still referenced regularly (three to five times a year) and in meteoritical circles my reputation still starts with being the first author of that paper.

The mystery of the origin of eucrites had been solved. Indeed, the mystery of the origin of meteorites in general, as pieces of the asteroid belt, was also resolved in part by this work.

But years later, studying philosophy as a part of my Jesuit training, I found a totally different mystery story that this paper's history could help me solve.

A great debate rages between different schools of thought in the field of philosophy of science on how scientific work is actually done. Reading about this debate made me wonder which side came closest to describing how I actually did my science. Whose philosophical theory best matched the history of my eucrite work?

Consider the group who call themselves *logical positivists*. Theirs was the classical way of viewing science; they insisted that scientific deductions progress via symbolic logic. By the use of logic, proofs are rigorous; by basing proofs on objective observations, one guarantees that the laws of science, so proved, do in fact correspond to reality. Like *Star Trek*'s Mr. Spock, they insist that logic and objective observation are independent of personalities, so psychology or sociology can't possibly be important to the logic of the science; to the extent that these impinge on the scientific work, the work is less than logical, or less than objective, and so less than scientific.

That's the model of science that most of us probably learned as kids . . . too often intoned in a stentorian voice from the ceiling, announcing What Science Tells Us. According to this school, progress is made: (1) by observation of nature, (2) by the development of a general rule which is hypothesized to explain the observation, (3) by the deduction of another possible consequence of that rule, and (4) by the use of that deduction to test the hypothesis from which the truth or falseness of the rule can be induced.

In my eucrite work, the mineralogy of the eucrites and the REE abundances observed in them could be said to constitute Part 1, Stolper's model is Part 2, the predicted REE abundances are Part 3, and the comparison of those abundances are Part 4. Thus, the model of doing science can be matched to the history of my project.

However, this way of looking at science ignores all the nonrational events—the coincidences of who it was that I happened to know and what they taught me—that figured importantly in the development of the eucrite work. More embarrassingly, it misses explaining the most important part of the eucrite work: the identification of Vesta as the source of the eucrites.

Historicism was a midcentury reaction to the logical positivist viewpoint. According to historicists like Thomas Kuhn, science is a human phenomenon based on human values and judgments. A model of reality is accepted by the society of scientists; puzzles are examined within the framework of this *paradigm* (one of their favorite words, and one that has almost been clichéd to death as a result). A severe failure of this paradigm, coupled with the appearance of a new paradigm, results in a *paradigm shift,* a scientific revolution to a new model.

All observations are "theory-laden," they say. It isn't possible to have "objective data" in the sense of the logical positivist view, because in order for data to be intelligible, they must fit into a theory. Thus, say the historicists, the logical positivists' link between their logic and reality is broken.

Indeed, more extreme views of this school go even further in describing the sociology of science. They say that each paradigm is accepted by a carefully controlled priesthood of science to the exclusion of all other paradigms. The puzzles that scientists solve don't have to have any direct relationship to reality; they mean something only in terms of the paradigm itself. And the success in solving a puzzle is merely how well the proposed solution fits into the sociology of those who work within the paradigm.

Thus, their procedure of science might be outlined as: (1) gain entry into the approved circle of science-doers, (2) find a puzzle amenable to solution of interest to those in the circle, and (3) using the logic and background preconceptions of the circle, derive a logically self-consistent solution to the puzzle.

Historicists could find in my story plenty of instances to support their point of view. The Lewis equilibrium condensation theory, which provided the conceptual framework to make the whole work possible, is about as clear an example of a paradigm as I know of in my field. Furthermore, the acceptance of my work was clearly for sociological reasons as much as rational ones. It came with the proper pedigree, it satisfied the politics of the moment, and it fit preconceptions (paradigms) that many scientists had already decided they wanted to believe in.

However, in detail there are some flaws with the historicist take. For instance, the Lewis "paradigm" was actually not particularly well known or understood outside of his circle.

And there was the Wasserburg question: did I, or did anyone, believe that my results really described the truth? Even 20-odd years later, and well aware of all the flaws in this specific work, I think it is fair to say that almost everyone in the field honestly believes that Vesta is covered with materials that look and evolved much like the basaltic meteorites, even if not everyone is convinced that Vesta is the only source for these meteorites. We in the field don't care that it fits someone's "paradigm;" we care that it is true.

Historicism, with its cynical distrust of authority, was obviously a child of the 1960s; and, like the 1960s, it produced its own yuppie reaction 10 years later. *Historical realism* is a view that accepts the sociological insights of historicism, yet still maintains that science has some validity in describing reality. As the historical realist will point out, whether science is valid or not doesn't depend on the purity of its philosophical bases, or in its conformity to its sociological setting, but whether it actually succeeds at predicting and explaining nature.

Think of the light bulb. The logical positivists could say that its invention followed logically and inevitably from the experiments of Franklin and Volta. The historicists may point out that Thomas Edison owed much of his success to the financial acumen and machinations of his backers, for instance, in founding and marketing the

General Electric Company. But the historical realists remember that Edison also owed his success to the fact that, when you flipped the switch, the light came on.

If you admit that science actually works (at least to some extent), you then have to explain why. The difficulty with historicism, in this view, is that it attempts to show why science ought *not* to work—a situation which is not, in fact, what actually happens in real life.

Science is rational but mutable, according to the historical realist. Changes occur, but they are guided by the content of the theory itself. Thus, the changes are justified because they allow one to come closer to the truth.

The first task for the historical realist is to define the "approved circle" of scientists in a less cynical way than an extreme historicist might do. Such a circle is a sequence of theories centered around a person, a discipline, or a key idea, formed when one collects concepts and separates them into well-defined "domains." Unlike the historicists, there is not one overwhelming paradigm that everyone agrees to follow, nor even only one paradigm per "domain." Each discipline changes, and the changes are driven both by the content of the domain itself and also with an eye to other disciplines. New ideas are developed and tested by both reason (intellectual factors) and social acceptance (professional factors).

Within a domain, progress is measured not in terms of how close it gets to the truth itself (unlike the logical positivists), nor by its ability to solve ultimately irrelevant puzzles (unlike the historicists) but rather by its ability to solve problems—that is, to solve puzzles that really do matter, to some degree, because they do have something to do with the truth.

How does one do science on a day-to-day basis, according to this school? Within a program/domain, the scientist:

1. Collects background information by observation of nature; such observations are still "theory-laden" but nonetheless can be objective.
2. Then a new hypothesis is introduced when the factual situation observed in part 1 cannot be explained by the old hypothesis.

3. The new hypothesis is accepted if it is both coherent and consistent within the domain, and with other domains. (For example, a solution to explain a chemical reaction that did not account for the laws of conservation of mass or energy would be rejected, even though those laws are in the domain of physics, not chemistry.)

Perhaps even more than most fields, because it began as an interdisciplinary field and is still very young, planetary science definitely can be fit into this mold. It consists of sets of theories centered around particular problems or persons. The question of the reflectance spectra of Vesta is in quite a different category from the measuring of REE abundances in meteorites. Both are separate from the questions of mineral formation and evolution. Each field has its own tools and its own goals. Because (especially in the 1970s) most practitioners of planetary science entered the field from ordinary geology, or physics, or astronomy, the sense of separate domains was quite strong.

Further, the historical realist view of data as objective, even though theory-laden, describes well the way that data were used in the eucrite case. By interpreting the results of neutron activation as giving abundances, by normalizing these abundances to cosmic abundances, by interpreting measured trace element abundances in laboratory samples in terms of partition coefficients, we were carrying ourselves far away from the raw data. And yet the meaning of the data remained clear. In my judgment the final numbers we used were meaningful. They were also uncertain, to some degree, but that was never denied or ignored. Our conclusions were kept weak—"consistent with the hypothesis that . . ."—for that very reason.

One serious flaw in the historical realist view of our science is that the real progress did not occur in order to solve a problem. It was never our intent to try to use geochemistry to link eucrites with Vesta, for the simple reason that we had thought the spectral reflectance work was already sufficient. It was an unspoken assumption to us that these meteorites came from Vesta. We were as surprised as anyone when we realized that this connection could be made, and that strictly speaking there was a need for such a connection.

Yet, unlike historicism or logical positivism, pushing the basic ideas of historical realism a bit further does allow us to understand how we came to this insight.

The story of the eucrites can be thought of as demonstrating what happens when different domains interact. The eucrite case saw the interaction of three distinct domains: the modeling of basalt formation, the chemical origin of the solar system, and spectral reflectance astronomy. The rival University of Oregon group did not overlap domains, and so even though they were able to solve the more limited problem of allowed starting conditions for the eucrites, they missed the connection to a Lewis-model solar system or the connection to Vesta. To them, one assumes the question of where in space these lavas were formed was something that they did not consider important, in the sense that they did not realize an answer to that question could be obtained by geochemical modeling.

Indeed, once the geochemical connection between Vesta and eucrites was made, the field was changed forever. Understanding the origins of extraterrestrial lavas was seen as a pointer, a fiery finger, to how geochemical modeling could connect meteorite samples with their planet of origin. The writing was on the wall. In the late 1970s, the first samples of unusual basaltic meteorites from the Antarctic ice were shown, on geochemical grounds, to be identical to Moon rocks. And another dozen basaltic meteorites have since been identified, again purely on geochemical arguments, as samples of Mars.

THE VINDICATION OF MARS

IN AUGUST of 1996, I
was traveling from Castel Gandolfo back to Tucson, and stopped over
for a few days in Long Island to visit some old friends from my MIT
postdoctorate days. Dan Davis had written a book with me, and he
and Léonie had been there to hear me out when I was trying to decide
whether to enter the Jesuits. Their home was just the place to spend a
couple of sticky summer days before heading back into the scientific
fray.

We were sitting around the table finishing the last bits of lunch
when the phone rang. Léo was closest, and picked up the receiver. A
funny look came on her face.

"Guy?" she said. "It's for you. It's a reporter named Woodward."

Bob Woodward? From the *Washington Post?* What could he possibly want . . .

I picked up the phone. "Hello, Guy?" asked a pleasant voice on the other end. "This is Kenneth Woodward. I'm the religion editor at *Newsweek*."

Oh. That Woodward. Actually, I had heard of him; he'd written a very good book about how the church goes about canonizing saints. But I didn't think that sainthood was why he was calling now. Rather, I suspected . . .

"I'm on vacation in upstate New York," he told me, "and my editor has just called. He says that they've found a meteorite from Mars that has evidence of life in it. Do you have any idea what this is all about?"

Ah, yes, just as I had suspected. Granted, I didn't know any more of the facts, at that point, than what had appeared on the TV news over the previous 24 hours. But I knew enough about meteorites, including Martian meteorites, to put it all into context. I did my best to explain it to him.

"Thanks," he said when I was done. "But the real reason I'm calling is to ask you, as a member of the Vatican Observatory, about the religious significance in this finding."

I thought for a microsecond. "None that I can see."

"Hmm," he replied. "That's kind of what I thought, too. But my editor says I have two columns to fill by five o'clock."

So we chatted a bit more about the vagaries of editors, and the ignorance of most journalists when it came to both science and religion. I gave him the names of two scientist friends, both religious believers, who I knew would be willing to be quoted in the press. Finally, we came back to the original question.

"The science is surprising," I said. "But there's nothing surprising, from a religious point of view, about God creating life elsewhere. God can do whatever He wants. That's the whole point of being God."

"All right," he said. "But can you phrase that in a way that I can quote?"

"Sure," I answered. "How about . . . uh, 'Finding life on another planet is merely an indication of God's creative power.'"

"Sounds good to me," he said.

I thought so, too; it felt like a perfect sound bite, carrying a certain air of profundity without really saying much of anything.

A couple hours later, he called back, checked over the story, read back my quote, and even checked the spelling of my name. I was impressed at the pains he took to get the details right.

"That's it, then," he said. "I'll write it up, then call the office down in New York and phone it in. It should be out on the stands next week."

So the following week, with great anticipation, I rushed out to see my name in *Newsweek*. Fumbling through the pages, I turned to see how they'd handle the story. When I found it, I nearly dropped the magazine.

"A Vindication of God!" ran the headline. Huh?

How could God be "vindicated"? What fool had said that? That made utterly no sense.

I read further. "Finding life on another planet is a *vindication* of God's power!" said someone named Guy Consulmagno. Whoever he is. Can't be me; I don't spell my name that way . . .

For all of Kenneth Woodward's efforts, the story had come out wrong. The preconceptions of the editors in New York had overpowered the actual story that he had phoned in.

It's not only journalism that has to fight preconceptions.

In the early 1990s I coauthored a textbook on planetary sciences, and included a homework question that ran something like this: "An interstellar probe discovers a star with two terrestrial planets. One has an atmosphere 99 percent carbon dioxide, 1 percent water. The other has an atmosphere 40 percent argon and 40 percent neon, both inert gases, and 20 percent fluorine (the most chemically reactive element in the periodic table). Which planet do you think is more likely to have life?"

I was trying to fight the preconception that carbon dioxide equals life, and teach the idea that life, as we knew it, was a process of enormous chemical disequilibrium. It's something that drives the chemistry of a planet's surface and atmosphere well away from simple thermal equilibrium and into a realm where horribly reactive elements like fluorine—or oxygen, which is the *second* most reactive element in the periodic table—might actually exist in copious amounts. That's how we'd seen life operate on Earth. The Gaia principle proclaims that in one sense, the entire Earth is "alive" because life on Earth is a complex interplay of billions of different systems, including a radical disequilibrium between the atmosphere and the surface.

All that oxygen in our atmosphere is why iron rusts, why we need fire departments, and why life can thrive. The picture was clear back then. Any planet with life would have an atmosphere way out of whack with what chemical equilibrium would predict. And once life had a toehold, it would hold on relentlessly, inexorably and irreversibly changing the surface of a planet. That was Earth.

By comparison, we knew Mars had a boring carbon dioxide atmosphere. Its air was in complete equilibrium with its rocks. Clearly it had no life. Clearly, it never had life. It had not suffered that inexorable, irreversible, Gaialike change.

So we knew that there was no life on Mars. And that's one reason why the report of microbe fossils in the Martian meteorite ALH84001 was received with enormous skepticism in the field.

But what if there really was life there?

My friend Dan Britt once expounded on his "three laws of geology" to me. "The first law of geology," he explained, "I learned when a professor on a field trip pointed out to us an elaborate history of mountain formation from the pattern of rocks, exposed where they'd cut a road through the side of a hill. The detail he came up with was remarkable. And since he'd taught us the theory of how that was all supposed to work, we could see it there, too. But I realized my first law: 'I would never have seen it, if I hadn't believed it.' "

The scientists at the Johnson Space Center in Houston were not the first to study rock ALH84001. They weren't the first to measure carbon or carbon isotopes, or to look closely at the thin disks of carbonate that had grown in cracks in the rock. They weren't the first to puzzle over the rims, zones of black and white and black that reminded some of an "Oreo cookie." Papers on all these topics were published in *Science* and *Nature* before they made their announcement. But they were the first scientists to look at this rock with the *belief* that it might show signs of ancient life.

If there had been life on Mars, where would you expect to find evidence for it? In the oldest sample, because it's the oldest surface features visible on Mars today that suggest it once had a thicker atmosphere than it has now, it once had warmer temperatures at its surface, it once had liquid water. Such evidences are mostly seen in heavily cratered ancient highlands. How ancient? We don't know; but judging by analogy with similarly cratered plains on the Moon we'd guess three billion years ago or so. All the Mars meteorites but one are younger than that. So you study the one old one.

That old one, ALH84001, about 4.5 billion years old, was a basalt—the kind of rock you'd expect from a volcano—that had been severely altered over time. One alteration visible even to the naked eye was the presence of little orange and white disks of carbonate. On Earth, carbonate is made by precipitation from a saturated fluid, or by living creatures. So that was an obvious place to look for evidence of bugs that might have lived in those fluids, bugs that might have contributed to the carbonate.

But the Martian carbonates were chemically different from Earth carbonates. The sorts of chemistry we're used to dealing with on Earth, and the kinds of conditions that produce these minerals, almost certainly don't apply on Mars. People are still arguing whether the Mars carbonates were formed at very high temperatures from a carbon dioxide gas, or from not quite so hot super-saturated water, or from cold water; whether it happened slowly, as a Martian lake evaporated, or quickly in the shock of a meteorite impact. Indeed, some workers have at one time suggested one theory and at the next meeting proposed a totally different scenario. We just don't know.

When Dave McKay, Kathy Thomas-Keprta, and Everett Gibson saw little wormlike structures in images from a new state-of-the-art electronic microscope, they thought they'd hit pay dirt. They went looking for other signs of fossilized life. And they thought they'd found it. They saw iron sulfides, just like bacteria make. They sent a sample off to Richard Zare at Stanford, without telling him what it was, and he found complex polycyclic aromatic hydrocarbons—stuff like you'd find from rotting dead life forms. They looked closely into the grains and found sheets of carbon-rich material that reminded them of biofilms, the product of bacteria. And in the carbonates they found magnetic grains of oxidized iron, magnetite, of a consistent size and shape and structure and purity that in any terrestrial rock would be accepted as proof of the presence of bacteria.

But hardly anyone believes them.

Now mind you, this is not a case where McKay and his colleagues are being accused of fraud or trickery. This isn't cold fusion. No one doubts their data. No one questions their images. But those who don't see any evidence of life in their results, are those who don't believe their interpretations.

The so-called bacteria are too small, they say. The skeptics point out that we're dealing at a scale, billionths of a meter, where even Earth rocks have not been well examined or understood. Some people see similar "nanobacteria" in Earth rocks, but others completely dispute the interpretation that these entities were, or were formed by, living creatures. And this is for Earth rocks; how can we believe it on Mars rocks?

The skeptics show their own microphotographs with extruded minerals in shapes reminiscent of the early McKay images, and point out that many of the so-called bacteria could actually be mineral grains. They point out that lots of processes, including terrestrial contamination, could be responsible for the life-hinting carbon abundances. They point out that lots of processes make iron sulfide, lots of processes make magnetite crystals. When you look at these images, these data, with the eyes of disbelief, you can find plenty of reasons not to believe. If you believe that the evidence is *not* of life, that's what you'll see.

If that's the case, how can anyone ever decide what's true? How can you ever change someone's mind?

New data would help. Today we can measure the carbon or sulfur isotopes of spots only a few micrometers across (and when we do, the results are not what we would expect for bacterial products). But to know for sure we're measuring the purported life stuff, and not just the surrounding rock, we need to be able to measure spots 10 or 100 times smaller. We can see wormlike fossils that maybe are made up of individual segments; if we could see 10 times finer, maybe we could see the cell walls of those segments.

But Dan Britt has a second law of geology: "Proof is always just beyond your limit of resolution." Now note that his first law didn't doubt the validity of the observation; it just pointed out that you had to be looking for something before you could see it. But this second law is worse; it says that by hoping too hard, you can fool yourself into seeing things that maybe are there, maybe aren't. And worse, you'll never be satisfied . . . because you'll always think that just one more experiment will prove what you're trying to prove. That way lies madness (and a thesis that never gets finished).

So what really does convince people to change their minds? What will settle this issue of ancient life on Mars?

It might be useful to examine a previous case, where people really did change their minds. It's one related to this whole issue: the question of how we know these "Mars" meteorites really come from Mars.

Let's put them in perspective. We have about 15,000 meteorites in our collections. Of these, only a few hundred look like chunks of basalt—frozen lava from some extraterrestrial volcanic event. But virtually all of those 15,000 meteorites, including virtually all of the basalt ones, were formed 4.6 billion years ago. We know this from the radioactive decay products inside the meteorites. And virtually all of them have metallic iron present, which means they came from some environment that was low in oxygen. These rocks were never rusted.

However, about a dozen meteorites—one in a thousand—are different. They're basaltic; but unlike the other basalts, they all have magnetite and other kinds of "rusted" iron present. Most have carbonate minerals, too . . . implying that not only oxygen but also carbon dioxide was present wherever they came from.

We know they don't come from the Moon, or the Earth. The isotopes of elements like oxygen in these rocks are distinctly different from Earth rocks, and outside of a nuclear reactor there's no easy way of changing Earth rock isotopes into isotopes like theirs.

And most of these meteorites have young ages. Yes, ALH84001 is old, 4.5 billion years; but it's the only one of this class with such an old age. Half of the others are just over a billion years old; and the rest are only a few hundred million years old! These are lavas that came from volcanoes that were active only a few hundred million years ago.

Now, no asteroid has active volcanoes today. Even the Moon's volcanoes were frozen up by 3 billion years ago. So these rocks must have come from a body more active, more recently, than our Moon.

How do you manage to heat a body enough to melt lava in its interior? The moons of Jupiter, especially Io, warm themselves because they are squeezed and distorted by orbiting so close to Jupiter's massive gravity field. That won't work for asteroids or planets. For most bodies, you need the slow decay of radioactive elements like potassium-40 and uranium to provide the heat.

Radioactive elements give off heat as they decay. But by the very fact that they are decaying, that means there's less and less of them available as time goes by. There may have been enough uranium and potassium in the Moon to produce basalts three and a half billion years ago, but today only about a tenth of the original radioactive atoms are left to produce heat.

At that rate, you need a pretty big planet to have enough radioactive atoms to keep its interior molten for four billion years. The Moon's too small; it's long been frozen up. So is Mercury. When you look around the solar system, the only real candidates that suggest themselves as sources for these young basaltic meteorites are Venus and Mars. Only they are big enough to possibly have active volcanoes so late in their history.

But how could you get a meteorite off Venus? Its gravity is almost as strong as Earth's, plus you have that whopping big atmosphere to get through. Any impactor would be slowed down before it could reach the surface; anything knocked off the surface would be slowed down further by that same atmosphere, before it could get into space.

Mars is much more likely. But could the impact of some large chunk of asteroid into Mars really knock a piece of the Martian crust off and launch it into space?

Nothing in our experience, no bomb and no volcano, has ever produced that much energy on Earth. We're flying blind when we try to estimate how the surface of a planet reacts to a really big impact. But we see craters on the Moon, and we see how far stuff gets tossed away from those craters. The bigger the crater, the farther stuff gets tossed. We can extrapolate from that, alter the equations to account for the higher gravity on Mars, and calculate that . . .

It's impossible.

Any impact big enough to launch stuff off Mars would have to be so big that it would destroy the crustal rock, melt it completely, before it ever got launched. And it'd leave a whopping big crater behind, the likes of which we do not see on Mars. It just plain didn't happen. And I can show you the numbers to prove it.

That's where the situation stood in the early 1980s. On the one hand, the chemists couldn't think of any place but Mars where these rocks could come from; on the other hand, the physicists said it was impossible.

Then in 1983 Don Bogard and Pratt Johnson at the Johnson Space Center in Houston looked more closely at one of these meteorites, EET79001, which had veins and blobs of glass ("nodules") running through it—lava that had been remelted when it was hit and launched into space, then quick-frozen before it had a chance to recrystallize. Within those veins were bubbles of gas. By some very careful lab work, they were able to extract the gas from those bubbles and measure its composition. In every detail it matched the composition of the Martian atmosphere as measured by the Viking landers back in 1976.

Now you have to know that, in a lot of ways, the Martian atmosphere had puzzled people, because its composition was very unusual. The elements and isotopes were in abundances that implied an extensive and complicated evolution. So finding these same odd abundances in a rock was pretty conclusive. Either this rock came from Mars, or it came from a body exactly identical to Mars in every detail . . . and Mars is the only Mars we know.

But what about the physicists' arguments? Dan Britt's third law of geology handles that one. "If it *did* happen," says Dan, "then it *can* happen."

Sure enough, with a little more computer time, the modelers figured out that maybe the structure of Mars is a little more complex than the Moon, and if you can focus seismic waves off layers and . . . well, the point is, the new calculations show it was possible after all for relatively small impacts to lift meteorites off the Martian surface.

Today virtually everyone in the field agrees that these meteorites came from Mars. So what changed people's minds? The gas measurements, right? Well yes, but that misses the point. The gas measurements were the capper, the missing piece; but they were significant, and convincing, precisely because all the other pieces of the puzzle—the state of the iron, the presence of carbonate, the young ages—had already been assembled. The gas measurements fit into a whole structure of knowledge that already existed.

That's exactly what is lacking so far with the life question. We really don't know enough about the chemistry at the surface of Mars, especially in its past, and we certainly don't know enough about life and how it starts and how it evolves to be able to make sense of all the odd things we've started to find in ALH84001. (And we're finding odd things in other Mars rocks, too, now that we've started looking.)

To accept that it's life, with no question, would mean throwing away a lot of what we previously thought we understood about how life takes hold and alters the environment of a planet. Mars today looks just like we always expected a sterile planet to look. If Mars is not sterile, our faith in our understanding of planetary chemistry is seriously shaken.

And furthermore, as near as we can tell the crystals where the purported bacteria fossils are found were formed just a bit after the rock itself was formed, some 3.9 billion years ago. If they really are fossils, they are older than any known life on Earth. If Mars harbored life in that far-distant past, even before Earth did, then our whole idea of how life got started will have to be rethought.

In the face of that, no one piece of evidence, even a hard-to-refute piece of evidence, by itself will completely turn the tables.

I emphasize this, because I think that in fact the NASA group have come up with a really hard-to-refute piece of evidence. Of all the arguments they've used, most of the press attention has been centered on the dramatic images of wormlike formations. But in many ways, that's the weakest of their evidence. Instead, it's those little magnetite crystals, the ones of a consistent size and shape and structure and purity, that are really hard to explain away. There's no known way to make them like that, except inside bacteria. So either nature's more clever than we thought at making magnetite without life, or they're somehow terrestrial contamination, or . . . they come from Martian bacteria.

And a lot of our ideas of planetary chemistry and the origins of biology go out the window.

But, if it did happen, it can happen.

Only a much broader understanding of Mars, including sample returns—plural—and maybe even including manned missions, will give us enough other pieces to figure out how these bugs fit into a larger picture.

Only a whole complex suite of evidence and theory can provide the kind of vindication of life that no one will argue with.

PART TWO

THE CONFESSION OF A VATICAN SCIENTIST

PRECURSORS OF EVIL

RECONCEPTIONS are
both the heart and the bane of science. When a preconception turns
out to be wrong, we mock it as prejudice. When it turns out to be
right, we call it insight.

The Church has certainly suffered its share of attacks for stub-
bornly holding onto its preconceptions. Everybody knows how
Galileo was persecuted by the Church for supporting the Copernican
theory of the planets orbiting the Sun. Everybody knows that the old-
fashioned theory of planets and Sun going around the Earth, due to
Ptolemy, was plainly wrong, and in the light of Galileo's proofs was
rejected by all clear-thinking scientists. And everybody knows how,
nonetheless, the Church could not bear to see the Earth displaced as
the center of the universe, because it threatened the central role in the
universe of humanity and God (and the Church itself).

Of course, everybody also knows that what everybody knows ain't necessarily so.

If the medievals adopted the Ptolemaic system as a way of illustrating the moral order, it was only to emphasize that the Earth was *not* the center of the universe, but the lowest link in the chain of creation. (And their imagery was, after all, based on the best science of their day. Who's to say if people in the year 3000 will laugh at those who'd use the big bang as the basis of their religious beliefs? Today's up-to-date is tomorrow's out-of-date.)

Actually, the Copernican system, as Copernicus himself presented it, was only marginally simpler than the Ptolemaic system. His planets did not go around the Sun in simple circles, but traveled around the average position of the Sun with epicycles and off-center circles, just like Ptolemy used. They had to; that's the only way he could approximate the actual positions of the real planets in the sky . . . Kepler's insight that orbits are elliptical was nearly a hundred years in the future.

Incidentally, after Copernicus published his book—at the urging of a churchman, Cardinal Nicholas von Schoenberg—in 1542, it was highly esteemed for the next 50 years because of its improved predictions of planetary positions. They were used to work out the reform of the calendar, by the Church, in 1582. But his tables were superseded by the improved observations of Tycho Brahe at the end of the century. At that point, the Copernican work was considered by most astronomers to be obsolete.

Tycho Brahe was probably the greatest pre-telescope observer of planetary positions (his tables were the data on which Kepler built his Laws of Planetary Motions). Tycho knew and respected Copernicus's work, but decided that the scientific evidence ultimately argued against a heliocentric system. Given the state of science in 1600, it's hard to fault his judgment. Kepler's Laws were 20 years in the future, and Newton's Laws of Physics more than 80 years down the road. Without both of those major advances, the Copernican system physically didn't make sense.

Why? To take just one example, Tycho asked: Why don't the positions of the stars appear to shift back and forth as the Earth goes around the Sun? Tycho had measured the positions of stars at different seasons of the year to a few arc-minutes of precision—around one part in 10,000—without seeing any such shift. Either the stars were incredibly far away, or else the Earth didn't move. It was generally believed, by Copernicus and others, that the stars were embedded in an icy sphere surrounding the solar system, and that they shine by reflected sunlight. Tycho calculated that if they were so distant as to show no motion, stars shining by reflected sunlight would have to be absurdly large to be as bright as they were. His observations and his calculations were correct. Only his model for the origin of starlight was incorrect. (It would take a hundred times better resolution—impossible without a telescope—to detect the apparent motion of the stars from the Earth's revolution around the Sun.)

This was the state of astronomy when Galileo began to publish his observations, and these are the preconceptions against which his work was judged. When we look at the nature of Galileo's "persecution" by the Church, we see where the preconceptions—indeed, misconceptions—are the most dangerous. Don't misunderstand me—what happened to Galileo was wrong, the Church was to blame, and it is important not to downplay the significance of the Church's faults . . . or its apologies. But if we don't see clearly what its real crime was, we are more likely to defend ourselves against the wrong sin, and let a terrible history repeat itself.

You could fill a library with all the books written about the Galileo affair, each one uncovering a different "key" to understanding what really went on, and who the real bad guys were. In fact, the whole story of why the Church let itself be used to go after Galileo will probably never be fully understood, because it is impossible to re-create all of the circumstances that surrounded the whole affair. It is possible, however, to draw some parallels between Galileo's times and our own.

In a funny way, modern astronomy has become so full of spacecraft and computer-aided images that we no longer instinctively identify those pretty pictures on the screen with the lights in the nighttime sky. Our remove has paradoxically made us emotional innocents when we go outside at night and see the real thing. When we escape light pollution, we can look up at a dark clear night with eyes no different from Galileo's, and be astonished in just the same way he was.

When I was a graduate student in the 1970s, studying the solar system at the Lunar and Planetary Laboratory in Arizona, I knew all about comets. I could quote the facts and figures, write the equations that described their comas and tails, and explain in painful detail their interactions with the plasma of the solar wind. I had that stuff down cold. So when my friend Bob Howell suggested that I might want to get up at four in the morning to actually see a real comet, Comet West, rising in the east, I honestly saw no reason to lose any sleep over it.

But, by chance, I did wake up the next morning about 4 a.m. After a grumbling debate with myself, I decided to pull on my jeans and go outside to take a look. The Arizona morning was chilly, the stony driveway around our low-rent house was hard on my bare feet, but I dragged myself out the front door, around the side of the house, and looked to the east.

And gasped.

It was simply the most stunningly spectacular sight in the sky I have ever seen. It was as big and bright as a photograph on a planetarium ceiling. Five times as big as Comet Hale-Bopp. I would not call it impressive; I would call it frightening. In a world where the regularity of the stars is one of the few things that can be counted on, the presence of this flamboyant looming stranger shook me to my core. I now understood why humankind has always seen comets as portents of evil.

Most of America missed Comet West. It came without much warning or fanfare, was around for only a week—a week mostly cloudy back east—and visible only in the wee hours. I had had this soul-shaking experience, and no words could describe to my friends back east what they had missed.

It was more than 20 years before I could even begin to repeat the experience. From Comet West in 1976 until Comets Hyukatake and Hale-Bopp in the late 1990s, a whole generation of amateur astronomers never knew what a good naked eye comet really could look like. For 20 years, comet astronomers had had to make do with faint objects easily seen only in telescopes. Thus, it is easy to understand the excitement and hype surrounding the appearance of Comet Hale-Bopp. Now imagine the excitement among the leading thinkers of the Renaissance when a series of three bright naked eye comets arrived in 1618. Up to then, it had been twice as long—more than 40 years—since any bright comet had been visible in European skies.

In 1619, the Jesuit priest Horatio Grassi of the Collegio Romano described them in a 10-page pamphlet, "An Astronomical Disputation on the Three Comets of the Year 1618." Writing soon after the invention of the telescope, he began by noting the recent advances in astronomy that the telescope had wrought.

> Unlike earlier generations, we are no longer bleary-eyed from continually watching the stars for portents since we know that they are very far removed from us. We have been able to distinguish the circular motions of Venus and Mercury; and who is not embarrassed to note that we see the Sun occasionally disfigured by spots? We have laid bare the stratagems of Mars in approaching the Earth, and we have exposed the attendants of Jupiter and Saturn, hitherto uselessly hidden away. Until now, only comets have remained aloof from these "lynx" eyes.

After discussing how the first two comets were difficult to observe—one was in Ursa Major in August when it is closest to the horizon, the second was "whitish, loose-textured, and of no considerable brightness"—the author continued,

> Finally, on the 29th of November, the sky carried a very bright comet upward from the east, of such brightness that all eyes and minds were immediately turned toward it, and great throngs gathered on mountains and other very high places.

With his observations of this comet, Grassi proposed

> to consider those things that are within the bounds of our knowledge . . . For I do not approach you today as the sinister crow or the evil screech owl, the precursor of evils from these comets forewarning of pestilences, famines, and the wars that they assist. If I merely explain the position, motion, and magnitude of those comets, I shall be satisfied that I have fulfilled my purpose.

All Grassi wanted to do was get a better idea of what a comet was.

Aristotle had maintained that comets were caused by gases rising from Earth that glowed by friction when they rubbed against the crystalline sphere that held the Moon. On the other hand, Tycho Brahe and Michael Maestlin, observing the Comet of 1577, had found by parallax that that comet was more distant than the Moon, and thus by inference comets must be objects out among the planets.

(The idea behind the parallax experiment was simple but elegant. Two observers at two different locations observe the comet at the same time, noting carefully its position relative to the stars. If the comet is close by—say, closer to us than the Moon—then the two observers will have sufficiently different angles on it that they'll see a difference in the comet's position. The size of this difference is its *parallax.* If the comet looks to be in exactly the same position to both observers, then it must be much farther from us than the Moon. The Moon was an important benchmark; anything inside its orbit was considered to be in the Earth's "sphere" and subject to local laws of physics, yet the Moon itself was close enough that observers in different places could just see a measurable parallax.)

But from 1577 until 1618 there had been no further naked eye comet visible in Europe. There was no way for others to see for themselves what a comet looked like. All they had were written reports and "artists' conceptions," the sorts of evidence that is very easy for a skeptic to discount (remember Thomas Jefferson and his attitude toward meteorites?) especially when they flew in the face of a well-established world view.

The issue of comets was especially important to seventeenth-century astronomers for several reasons. For one thing, if comets really were planetary bodies, their orbits were very odd. They did not pass through the zodiac with the other planets. They appeared to move in straight paths, but their rate of travel varied radically from place to place. Indeed, Tycho himself concluded that they might have oval-shaped orbits, in total contradiction to the accepted physics of the day. Did they cross the orbits of the other planets, through those crystalline spheres that, according to popular conception, every planet was embedded in?

More intriguing to Tycho, he was unable to see any sort of retrograde motion in the comet's orbit. Retrograde motion, the little "backwards dance" that all the superior planets appear to go through when the Earth is between the planet and the Sun might be caused by two things. The classical explanation, originating with Ptolemy and endorsed by Tycho, was that the planets circulated in "epicycles" about their orbits. The rival theory of Copernicus held that retrograde motion was actually the motion of the Earth—his one simplification to the Ptolemaic system.

If Copernicus was right, then every body orbiting the Sun outside the Earth's orbit should show retrograde motion at some time. But comets didn't. It was a major strike against the Copernican theory . . . unless, of course, it turned out that comets were not orbiting bodies at all, but merely local phenomenon like a rising ball of luminous gas erupting from the Earth itself.

So Grassi carefully measured the comet's position, and compared his measurements in Rome to those of colleagues further north in Austria. The result: no visible parallax. Indeed, both groups saw the comet occult a sixth-magnitude star in Boötes at the same time. Since one can see some parallax for the Moon, one knows that the comet must be much farther away than the Moon. It's not in the atmosphere. Bad news for Copernicus.

That was his first, and main, point. But in addition, Grassi noted that the comet's orbit was consistent with following a great circle on the celestial sphere, as one might expect for a body in a circular orbit around the Earth, and certainly not the kind of irregular motion one would expect from a fiery cloud of gas rising from the Earth. And indeed, given its distance, it's hard to imagine any sort of fire that could burn as bright for as long as the comet.

Furthermore, a line between the comet's head and the tip of its tail always pointed away from the Sun. Grassi concluded that the comet shone by reflecting the Sun's light. The curve of the tail was not a puzzle to him since, as he understood it, the laws of perspective used by artists said such a curvature is what you'd see by looking at a straight tail but at an odd angle. (He got this part wrong; but, in his defense, it should be noted that perspective was still a young science at that time.)

Grassi's third point was perhaps his most revolutionary—even though it, too, was ultimately not quite right. To get to it, he looked at the comet through a telescope: the first person to do so.

If perspective was still a young science, the telescope was in its infancy. It was only 8 years earlier that Galileo Galilei had written *The Messenger of the Stars*. With his telescope, for the first time Galileo had seen the disks of Venus and Mercury, changes in the apparent size of Mars as it approached the Earth, sunspots, the moons of Jupiter and the rings of Saturn; all the items listed in Grassi's introduction. In addition, for the first time the Milky Way was revealed to Galileo as a collection of individual, small stars.

Galileo, the champion of the telescope, was the leading light of an informal club of scholars who called themselves the Academy of the Lynxes, taking for themselves the traditional cleverness and sharp vision of the lynx. Hence the allusion where Grassi mentions that "only comets have remained aloof from these 'lynx' eyes." Galileo had not observed comets; until now, no comets had been available for him to observe.

The telescope itself was controversial. Yes, for the first time all the wonders of the sky could be seen; but also, for the first time, a scientist had to rely on some mechanical device in order to study nature. This was quite unsettling, especially to those who did not understand how the telescope worked. Plenty of people in Galileo's time were skeptical about the reality of his moons around Jupiter—especially since the best physics of the day insisted they shouldn't exist.

Thus, Grassi patiently explained how a telescope could be used to prove the distance of an object. He noted that

> when the comet was observed through a telescope, it suffered scarcely any enlargement. Nonetheless, it has been discovered by long experience and proved by optical reasons that all things observed with this instrument seem larger than they appear to the naked eye; but, according to the law that the enlargement appears less and less the farther away they are removed from the eye, it results that fixed stars, the most remote of all from us, receive no perceptible magnification from the telescope.

Therefore, since the comet appeared to be enlarged very little, it will have to be said that it is more remote from us than the Moon, since when this has been observed through the telescope it appears much larger.

I know that this argument is of little significance to some, but perhaps they have given little consideration to the principles of optics which, it must be understood, play a very important part in what we are considering.

Poor Grassi. For quite forgivable reasons, he bollixed up this argument completely. The magnifying power of a telescope stays constant, at any distance. (Astronomy would be a whole lot easier if Grassi's proposal were true; finding absolute distances to planets and stars has always been tricky, a problem that plays a key role in the Hubble constant debate to this day.)

The trouble is that, because of the wave nature of light—which no one would understand for another 200 years—there is a limit to how tiny an angle any given telescope can resolve. All stars are smaller than this resolution limit in any optical telescope, even the biggest ones built to date. A telescope of Grassi's day would do well to resolve an angle of 5 arc-seconds, but the closest star subtends less than 0.01 arc-second. Thus, to our eye stars appear as points; even in a well-focused telescope, they are still only points of light.

Grassi was correct in observing that the telescope cannot make stars look bigger. He leapt to the obvious, but wrong, conclusion that this was due to their distance, not their small size (in terms of the angle they subtend in the arc of the sky).

The nucleus of a comet, though much closer than a star, is also much smaller. At one astronomical unit away (the distance between Earth and the Sun), a 5-kilometer (km) comet nucleus would only be as big as a star at 4 light years. So it, too, is well below the resolution of Grassi's telescope and it, too, would look like a point of light. The coma and tail would look bigger, of course; but Grassi could be forgiven for thinking that his telescope was simply making some dimmer outer region of the coma and tail brighter and hence easier to see.

However, Grassi's final comment, "I know that this argument is of little significance . . ." was most unfortunate. For one thing, Grassi himself did not understand optics. To condescend to others in that manner was uncalled for. He, of course, was thinking of those people who didn't believe the telescope actually showed you what was really out there, those who had doubted Galileo's observations.

Grassi, like most of the Jesuits at the Roman College then, considered himself as a friend and defender of Galileo. The Jesuits were bitter intellectual rivals of the Dominicans (in an era where such affairs could lead to wars) and, after all, it had been a Dominican in Florence who first accused Galileo of heresy; that alone would be enough to rally Jesuits to his defense. But, in addition, they had been honestly excited and delighted by his discoveries. An aged Father Christopher Clavius, the Jesuit who had headed up the reform of the calendar under Pope Gregory 30 years earlier, had used and enthusiastically endorsed his telescope (though, like Brahe, he was not convinced by the Copernican system).

When Galileo himself saw Grassi's book, however, he thought this last jibe was aimed directly at him. And furthermore, Galileo had three strong emotional reasons for wanting not to believe in comets as distant, astronomical objects.

For one thing, as mentioned earlier, a real, distant comet caused problems for the Copernican theory. There was no retrograde motion. It never occurred to anyone that the aphelion of a comet—the farthest point in its orbit, where the retrograde motion occurs—would be so far off that the comet would be unseeable. By the time a comet becomes visible, it is moving faster than Earth and so no retrograde motion occurs. In truth, all this might have been inferred from Kepler's laws, published in 1609, but no one but Kepler had really understood their significance yet. Galileo certainly didn't; he insisted on circular orbits to the end of his days.

A deeper problem for Galileo was that Tycho Brahe had used parallax to find the comet's distance. Galileo hated Brahe, and all he stood for, because Brahe's theory of the solar system was the most serious rival to Copernicanism at the time. Brahe's model held that the Earth was fixed, and the Sun went around the Earth, while all the other planets went around the Sun. In truth, no observation of planetary motions can distinguish between these two theories—they are, in fact, identical, with merely a change of origin from Sun to Earth. Further- more, Brahe's theory got around a lot of scientific problems that Copernicanism by itself couldn't handle. And it was consistent with the best physics of the day.

It was also politically safer. In 1619, thanks to the backlash against Galileo's earlier agitations, the original version of Copernicus' book had been placed on the index of restricted literature.

(Which raises a question for historians to ponder . . . given such a state of affairs, why did Galileo support the Copernican view so strongly, even back in the 1590s, some 20 years *before* his telescope? Indeed the heliocentric view did not gain wide acceptance for another 50 years after Galileo, when finally Newton's new physics was able to reproduce Kepler's laws—the Kepler solar system of elliptical orbits, not the strict Copernicus theory—from first principles.)

But finally, one can suspect a third reason why Galileo hated the idea of comets orbiting in space. He was, after all, the first person to see planets, stars, and nebulae through a telescope. He was extremely jealous of his priority in this regard. But he never observed the comet! In the fall of 1618, he later wrote, he was sick in bed. His string of firsts had been usurped. He wouldn't be the last astronomer to think he "owned" a certain field, and surely missing out on comets irritated him no end. The only salve to his pride would be to show that comets were not astronomical objects at all, but mere chimerae, bits of meteorology, refractions of light in the upper atmosphere of the Earth.

To this end, a thin book appeared in 1619: *A Discourse on the Comets*. The author, Mario Guiducci, was a friend and student of Galileo's.

After discussing, and dismissing, the opinions of Aristotle and other classical scholars on the origin of comets, and fulsome praise of Galileo (including a gratuitous slam at another Jesuit, Christopher Scheiner, who had dared to publish observations of sunspots at the same time as Galileo), Guiducci began his argument as to why the comet cannot be a body like a planet. First, he noted that a planet like

Mars gets noticeably brighter as it approaches Earth; "but a comet," he said, "is very large when it first appears, and afterward grows little or not at all for a very short time, subsequently diminishing during all its remaining period until . . . it is completely lost . . ." (One suspects that this is the work of someone who had not actually seen the comet; only in pretelescope days was it true that comets were "large" before they were first noticed.)

Second, he noted correctly the rarity of comets. If the comet of 1618 had appeared before, the earliest possible apparition would be the most recent bright comet (assuming, falsely, that all apparitions of a comet are equally bright) which was in 1577. But this, he argued, would require an absurdly huge orbit (which, in fact, we now know is the case and not so absurd after all). Furthermore, it would be completely inconsistent with a body in a circular orbit moving at a constant rate, since the comet itself was visible for such a short time, yet traversed such a large arc of the sky.

Of course, Kepler had already explained the irregular motion of bodies in elliptical orbits, with his second law in 1609. He had even sent a copy of his book to Galileo, but the latter never accepted Kepler's laws. (It's possible he never read the book; Kepler wrote in very difficult Latin, which Galileo—a university dropout—would have had a very hard time understanding.)

Guiducci then went on at some length to dispute the aristotelian view that comets are ignited by the friction of gases against the celestial spheres, arguing (incorrectly) that friction alone does not cause heat, and (again incorrectly) that fluids inside a sphere do not sense and are not moved by the rotation of the sphere.

Up to this point, little had been said directly contradicting Grassi's observations. In the second half of the discourse, however, Grassi's observations and theories were directly attacked.

First, Guiducci proposed that comets may simply be reflections of light in our atmosphere, not real objects. This, he asserted, would nullify the parallax argument. As an example, he pointed out that a rainbow will appear to move depending on the point of view of the observer; why not, likewise, a comet? (Again, one suspects that the author of this idea had never actually seen a comet. Nor, indeed, is the refraction argu-

ment logically worked out—unlike rainbows, comets show no preferred position relative to the Sun.)

He then went on to discuss Grassi's other two arguments in favor
of the comet's distance. As we have already seen, both are false, and
the author of the Discourse did not hesitate to point out their flaws.

First he attacked Grassi's mistaken argument concerning how the
telescope's magnification varies with the distance of the object being
observed.

> I had not intended to say anything about . . . this argument, since it
> appeared to me quite incorrect and false, and I did not believe it had
> gained assent except from persons of so little authority that it would
> not be worthwhile to consider it . . .
>
> . . . but mathematicians [at the Collegio Romano] had so high a
> regard for these arguments as not only to approve them, but to crit-
> icize those who had deprecated them, calling them little skilled in
> the principles of perspective and in the telescopic effects which they
> themselves had understood and observed by virtue of long experi-
> ence and from theorems of optics. This made me reconsider . . .
>
> Long before the appearance of the work mentioned, [Galileo]
> had contradicted that reasoning and deemed it worthless, more pos-
> itively and more publicly than anyone else.

Clearly the author of the *Discourse* saw himself the victim and wanted
his revenge.

What followed was a detailed, if somewhat confusing, description
of a telescope's operation. From his discussion of changing the telescope focus, and how he saw "halos" around bright objects, one gets the
impression that the author had a rather flawed telescope and perhaps
seriously bad eyesight. Both were true of Galileo. But the general thrust
of his argument, that Grassi's reasoning is flawed, is quite correct.

Discussing the supposed great circle motion of the comet, the
author showed that every comet would have to have its own celestial
sphere and the absurdity, to him, of so many individual orbits seemed
self-evident. Certainly, he pointed out, circular orbits are impossible.
Behind these self-evident absurdities he saw the absurdity of Brahe's
system itself, commenting that Grassi had

accepted the same hypothesis as Tycho; beyond the little which he has written in support of Tycho's opinion, I am led to affirm this by seeing how much he concurs with Tycho's other fantasies through the remainder of the work.

If the comet's orb is as these authors depict it, it is a great source of wonder to me that the Fathers at the Collegio have later been persuaded to call the comet the offspring of heaven; being in effect a triple goddess, it would have to be made an inhabitant of the heavens, of the elemental regions, and also of hell: since the elongation of our comet from the sun exceeded 90 degrees, a smattering of geometry suffices to show that if its orb encircles the Sun, it must, after running through the sky a long way, traverse the elements and then plunge into the infernal bowels of the Earth . . .

The sarcasm is evident, even if the argument is somewhat obscure and ultimately wrong.

Father Grassi was, by most accounts, a mild-mannered man, sensitive, a bit insecure; documents in the Jesuit archives describe him as having a "rather melancholy temperament," who suffered ill health most of his life. But his response to this criticism was anything but mild.

Perhaps part of his frustration with Galileo came from the restrictions against Copernicanism. The Copernican theory was appealing to many Jesuits: it was one of the evidences of the superior science of the west that the Jesuits brought to the court of the Chinese emperor, and Kepler was on excellent terms with the Jesuits. But the Jesuits had just come through a bitter debate of a point of theology with the Dominicans; their greatest (and most respected) theologian, Cardinal Bellarmine, had just died; and in short, at that moment they were in no position to get involved yet again in another protracted controversy. Where before they could compare the different cosmologies with an open mind, the impolitic agitation of Galileo had brought about exactly what they feared, political interference with their science.

You can almost hear a plaintive cry as Grassi defends his reliance on the Brahe system:

Is following Tycho such a crime? Whom instead should we follow? Ptolemy, whose followers' throats are threatened by the out-thrust sword of Mars now made closer? [The visible increase in the size of Mars in a telescope over the course of a year rules out the Ptolemaic system.] Copernicus? But he who is pious will rather call everyone away from him and will spurn and reject his recently condemned hypothesis. Therefore, Tycho remains as the only one whom we may approve of as our leader among the unknown courses of the stars.

This passage comes from *The Astronomical Balance,* a book supposedly written by Grassi's student Horatio Sarsi Saloniensi (writing under the anagram of Lothario Sarsi Singensano). In it, "Sarsi" attempts to put the arguments of Galileo in the balance, to see which side's reasons are the better. In it, he addresses Galileo directly, ignoring the fiction of Guiducci as author. The book is as long as the previous two combined, as Sarsi disputes point by point every subject, no matter how irrelevant, addressed in the *Disputation.*

Galileo says that one cannot ignite comets by friction? Sarsi provides counterexamples of how friction heats things. (Some are drawn from legends and are clearly ridiculous; in practice one cannot boil an egg by swinging it through the air, contrary to the Babylonian legends he quotes. Others, however, come from actual experience. Spinning eggs aside, his understanding of friction and heat is clearly better than Galileo's.) Never mind that the point is pointless, since Sarsi—and Grassi—never argued that comets were ignited by friction, either.

Do smooth spheres cause the air inside them to move when they spin? The answer is important only if you believe in the crystalline spheres of the planets, something neither party does; nonetheless, Sarsi argues that topic at length, too. (And, incidentally, he is closer to being correct than Galileo's side.)

More to the point, Sarsi made several strong and obvious arguments against the idea of the comet being a refraction of sunlight through a rising cloud of vapor. Galileo himself had said that the parallax of such an object should be that of the Sun, but Tycho's comet of 1577 had a measurable parallax and was clearly located at a distance greater than the Moon and less than the Sun.

On the matter of how a telescope works, Sarsi pointed out—quite correctly—that the telescope does two functions: it both makes small objects bigger and faint objects brighter. (By late 1619, when this book appeared, Grassi may well have received Kepler's book on Copernicus whose appendix carefully, and correctly, described the optics of a telescope. On the other hand, Galileo was never sent a copy of this book because he had never bothered even to acknowledge the other books Kepler had sent him.) Again, this served as an answer to an argument raised in the *Disputation,* but it was off the point. Grassi was still wrong in thinking that the lack of magnification in size proved the distance to the comet.

This second book made Galileo even angrier. In his copy of the book are notes in his handwriting calling Grassi and his arguments "oxen," "lousy buffalo," and "elephantine." His response was 3 years in the writing: Galileo's classic text on his philosophy of science, *The Assayer,* published in 1622.

The title is a pun in Italian contrasting fine jewelers' scales to Grassi's rough "astronomical balance." Galileo's *Assayer* was dedicated to his friend and fellow member of the Academy of the Lynxes, Matteo Barbarini, who had just been elected Pope. With a friend as Pope, and other close colleagues appointed to high places in the bureaucracy, Galileo felt confident that his time had come.

The book opens with an Imprimatur, the official pronouncement of the Church censor that the book was free of doctrinal error. But in this case, the censor, Nicolo Riccardi—a Dominican, to add further insult to the Jesuits—went even further, adding:

> Besides having found here nothing offensive to morality, nor anything that departs from the supernatural truth of our faith, I have remarked in it so many fine considerations pertaining to natural philosophy that I believe our age is to be glorified by future ages not only as the heir of works of past philosophers but as the discoverer of many secrets of nature which they were unable to reveal, thanks to the deep and sound reflections of this author in whose time I count myself fortunate to be born—when the gold of truth is no

longer weighed in bulk, in a mere set of scales, but is assayed with so delicate a balance.

Following this are several pages of embarrassingly rich praise, similar to the kinds of critics' acclaims one finds nowadays in the front pages of a Tom Clancy novel. Among them is a poem of 24 verses including such lines:

> *Glory must be yielded by*
> *those daring modern explorers, celebrated to the sky,*
> *who have charted unknown shores and newfound seas;*
> *you, however, add not just new lands here*
> *but in skies sublime you make appear*
> *new stars like these.*

As had become his custom, Galileo wrote the book in Italian for the popular audience, not in Latin for the scholars. Galileo made his living by selling books.

Historians of science have often described how this book influenced the philosophy of science for the next 200 years. Galileo demanded clear logic and experimental data rather than resting on the authority of ancient authors, with their spinning hard-boiled eggs. (Of course, one also may suspect that Galileo took personal offense at appeals to the ancients, as an aspersion on his less-than-complete classical education.) Likewise, the acerbic tone made it an entertaining best seller. It was a fun read—so long as you weren't on the receiving end of the acid.

The issue of the comet is supposedly the impetus for the book. Galileo pontificates on it, even though he admits he never saw it. But, ultimately, it plays only a minor role. Indeed, the entire introduction is dedicated to attacking every person, both the scoundrel and the honest scientist, who had dared to publish on Galileo's turf.

He even mocks Grassi hiding behind the name of a student; by contrast, he insists that the *Discourse* really was the work of his own student, Guiducci. (The original manuscript of the Guiducci work still exists. Most of it is in Galileo's handwriting.) And *The Assayer* contains enough scientific errors to embarrass even the most ardent Galileo supporter.

But to me the most striking aspect is the contrast in tone between *The Assayer* and Galileo's first astronomical work, *The Messenger of the Stars.* The *Messenger* is a book filled with light, with the joy and wonder of discovery; it is the work of a brilliant mind who could understand the things he was seeing for the first time through his telescope and, furthermore, understood their implications. Twelve years later, in *The Assayer* Galileo had become a querulous old man, more interested in scoring debater's points than in enjoying truth for its own sake.

Galileo's triumph in the success of *The Assayer* was a pyrrhic victory. With his sarcasm, his playing to the galleries, his out-and-out lies, he managed to permanently alienate the very people who might have been best positioned to defend him. Ten years later, when many of Galileo's friends in high places had died, the Pope found himself on the receiving end of his old friend's sarcasm. In the subsequent trial, the Jesuits stayed silent.

Finally, though, it is worth stepping back and noting the emotional climate surrounding the phenomenon that started it all: the comet itself. Both Galileo and Grassi reacted with deep emotion to this comet, and to the things the other said about it. Both were guilty of seeing in the comet only what they wanted to see. Both were influenced more by whom they liked than by what was true. And both of them behaved as if they, personally, had ownership of that part of the heavens.

Science has always had problems studying comets. The phenomenon is spectacular, short-lived, and rare. As a result, observations can sound unbelievable, while they are also unrepeatable. Skeptics cannot go back a year later and reobserve the object for themselves; by that time, the comet has returned to the outer reaches of the solar system. And one may have to wait years—41 years, in the case of Tycho's comet of 1577—before the next comet comes along. Even then, there is so much variation from comet to comet that one can never be sure that what was observed in one comet will necessarily be repeated in the next.

But it was the jealous, possessive attitude of Grassi and Galileo—all the more offensive for coming from supposedly calm and rational men of science—that caused the final breach. The ill feeling on both sides that led to Galileo's final trial in 1633 helped set back science in Italy for years, and has fed antireligious and antiscience bigots on both sides of the issue ever since. The rift between science and religion was as great a disaster as any of the famines and bloodshed that the ignorant, superstitious peasantry feared would come with the comet of 1618.

Coincidentally, 1618 marked the beginning of the Thirty Years War.

The Rift of
Popular Culture

HAT EXACTLY is this "rift" between science and religion?

The cliché is to speak of Godless science or of religion that fears truth. But a faith that fears the truth has no faith. And a philosophy with no God has no point . . . anyone dedicated to Truth is dedicated to the same God as the One who proclaimed Himself "the Way, the Truth, and the Life."

Indeed, "atheism" by itself is a slippery term. There are a whole lot of versions of religion that I don't believe in either; to a Hindu, or a Moslem, or a Fundamentalist, I probably look like an atheist, too. And while I certainly count among my friends and colleagues those who would call themselves "atheists," once I became a Jesuit I found to my surprise that an awful lot of my colleagues were eager to talk to me about their churches. Rather than being Godless, I'd say the proportion of churchgoers among scientists is not much different from that of the general public.

Yet there is a variety of atheist that is not content to search, in whatever way, for Truth. They are rare, but very vocal . . . to the embarrassment of most scientists. (Just as extreme fundamentalists embarrass most believers.) They are the ones who would turn science itself into their religion.

Those worshippers of science who want to beat up on the Church will always start with the Galileo affair. They have to . . . precisely because his trial was a unique event in Church history. Never, before or since, did the Catholic Church try to put a strict-construction interpretation on Biblical statements that might be relevant to natural science.

In fact, the whole tradition of Church teaching, including Origen, St. Gregory of Nyssa, St. Augustine, and St. Aquinas, is that the Bible is a book about God, not nature. It's a book that uses human language in a poetic way to describe things that ordinary language cannot contain. And there's the first rub to the science fundamentalists, the science literalists. They don't understand how poetry can express truth, why a metaphor can be stronger than a syllogism.

What is less effective is when religious thinkers try to illustrate and communicate religious ideas about transcendent things by using the language and concepts of the best scientific and historical knowledge to date. Unfortunately, this practice only weakens religious arguments, since it relies on knowledge that will inevitably go out of date as our understanding of the universe grows.

The "cosmology" of Genesis, for example, is not something that the author of Genesis invented. It was the standard cosmology, attributed to the Babylonians, at the time that Genesis was written (or at least, created orally), and one that the author could assume all his listeners were familiar with. Starting with this standard cosmology, the author added the "stuff" about God. But as the millennia passed and our scientific thinking developed, naturally this old cosmology became dated.

In fact, there are several different creation stories within Genesis itself that were obviously added at different times with different levels of cosmology. What's consistent is the idea that however you picture the universe being formed, it was the action of a creator God.

Yet these outdated images have not always caused an irreconcilable problem. The cosmology of Genesis was ancient and out of date even by the time of the Romans. It is, after all, not the cosmology of Ptolemy, but that of ancient Babylon. No one in first-century Rome still believed in a flat universe surrounded by "the waters" as described in the Psalms. But those Romans, unlike most twentieth-century atheists, were sophisticated enough to be able to read beyond the poetic words to the content they intended to convey. The "God stuff" that was new was still relevant, just in need of a new retelling.

It was only with the rise of literacy in the 1500s that a lot of people who knew (barely) how to read, but otherwise did not have much of a sophisticated education, started interpreting the Bible for themselves as if it were some sort of "magic book." And the more the Church tried to stop this sloppy theology, the more that the English (and thus anti-Roman) historians—on whom our culture is based—condemned the Church for restricting "freedom of thought."

The big problem for the newly literate was that the Bible seemed to say things directly contradicted by scientific evidence. For instance, geology demonstrated that the Earth must be millions of years old, while the Bible said it was created only 6000 years ago.

But wait a minute; that's not actually in the Bible. It's only the result of a foolish calculation by an English bishop in the 1600s. It was certainly never Catholic doctrine! Today it's become a "straw man" perpetuated by those who want to use Bishop Ussher as a stick to beat religion. And the sad result is that good people, told by these science-fundamentalists that they must choose between their religion and science, have felt forced away from embracing science.

But what about the very cause of the trouble that Galileo found himself in? Didn't the Church teach that the Earth was the center of the universe, and the Sun and everything else revolved around it?

Actually, that's neither in the Bible nor was it ever official Church teaching at any time—except implicitly during the brief period around the time of Galileo. Indeed, it was never debated at Galileo's trial, according to the official transcript. It was merely assumed, as a convenient stick to go after someone who was both unpopular and politically vulnerable. The prosecution of Galileo by the Church was a terrible crime, but it was not an attempt to define formally and dogmatically something that we now know to be untrue.

Despite its suppression of Galileo's ideas, the Church was never in the business of retarding the advancement of knowledge. On the contrary, it can be argued that it played a progressive role in the birth of modern science.

When thirteenth-century philosophers at the University of Paris rediscovered Aristotle they found that some of his ideas, like an unchanging universe without beginning or end, came in conflict with the Christian teaching of an omnipotent creator God. In 1277 the Bishop of Paris, Stephen Tempier, responded by listing 219 philosophical propositions that he banned from his diocese. Among them was the assertion that "God could not have made other worlds." God is omnipotent, the Bishop reasoned, and so we have to admit the possibility of "alternate universes." Even then, the Church encouraged philosophers to look beyond Aristotle.

In the 1300s, John Buriden and Nicholas Oresme, both churchmen, wrote about the possibility that the Earth could be moving and spinning nearly 300 years before Galileo. Even Copernicus's work was published nearly 100 years before Galileo, at the encouragement of a Cardinal, and, as we have seen, it was well regarded by the Jesuits. William Gilbert actively pushed Copernicanism in his book on the Earth's magnetic field 15 years before Galileo got started.

But when Galileo dusted off these ideas, and unlike Gilbert wrote about them in the common language of the people, pushing them like a seventeenth-century Carl Sagan in the fashionable salons of Italy, people were shocked. This fed the Renaissance (and modern) prejudice that the medieval times were a period of religious fundamentalism, some sort of dark age. In fact, it was a combination of bad Renaissance theology and bad Renaissance science that ganged up on Galileo; but it happened to him, and not any of his predecessors, because he was the first to push these ideas into the popular culture.

In contrast, for the rest of its history the Church has happily accepted the possibilities of alternative cosmologies. Even Cardinal

Bellarmine's letter to Galileo did not reject his theory on religious grounds, but simply noted that it was "not proved," which was certainly true at the time. In the end, Galileo was *not* condemned as a heretic; the crime he was convicted of was disobedience. (The actual documents of Galileo's case are available in English translation in a book edited by M. A. Finocchiaro, *The Galileo Affair*, University of California Press, 1989.)

Evolution is the other major issue that leads people to believe that science is incompatible with religious teaching. Again, it's important to distinguish between what fringe fundamentalists have said, and what is actual Catholic or other mainstream Christian teaching. The Catholic Church never formally condemned "evolution." Indeed, the only two times Popes spoke on the matter, in the 1940s and in Pope John Paul II's recent statement, it said just the opposite. They saw no conflict to religion in the theory of evolution, as long as one acknowledged God the creator acting in this way.

The denial of scientific knowledge is not a prerequisite of religious faith; nor is it necessary to deny the existence of God in order to pursue science. Albert the Great, father of geology; Roger Bacon, father of chemistry; Gregor Mendel, father of genetics; Christopher Clavius, the "second Euclid" of the Renaissance; Angelo Secchi, father of astrophysics; Georges Lemaître, inventor of the big bang theory . . . all were priests or monks. Indeed, up until the rise of the modern university in the nineteenth century, most scientists were in fact clergymen—they alone had the education, and the free time, to indulge in scientific pursuits.

Copernicus, Tycho Brahe, Galileo, Kepler, Newton . . . all considered themselves to be devout Christians. So did James Clerk Maxwell, whose theory of electromagnetism made possible the twentieth century, and Guglielmo Marconi, who used Maxwell's equations to make radio and its descendants possible. Einstein, though not aligned with any particular organized religion, valued his Jewish heritage and professed a devout theism. Buzz Aldrin, an Episcopal lay minister, brought the Eucharist to the Moon.

Historically there has been no cause for conflict between science and religion. The only clear example of such a conflict, the Galileo affair, occurred nearly 400 years ago; and the Church has repeatedly admitted its mistake on that score. So why does everyone still think a Church-science conflict exists? Why is it that in the popular culture, science and religion are thought to be opposed? To understand why, we need to look not at science, nor at religion, but at the popular culture.

Where do most people learn about religion? Where do they learn about science?

Religious education for most of us in the Christian faith begins and ends with Sunday school class; who studies religion past the age of 12? So many people leave the Church before they're old enough to appreciate it. It's no wonder they have only a childish view of religion . . . they only encountered it when they themselves were children.

The same phenomenon holds true with science. Most kids are turned off from science by the time they reach high school. You can always blame the teachers. But most grade-school teachers don't get a very good grounding in science at any point in their education; they didn't have good teachers, either. In college, science classes for education majors are usually huge lecture courses where hundreds of students are required to memorize many cheerful facts about the square of the hypotenuse. One survey has shown that you have to learn more new vocabulary words in freshman physics than you do in freshman French! (But science isn't memorizing facts, any more than religion is quoting verses from the Bible.)

Likewise, a distorted picture of both science and religion pervades the media today. News reporters and dramatists are only interested in conflict, in action, in—well—news and drama. Harmony and reconciliation don't make good box office; there's no story there. And so only the turmoil on the fringe of religions gets reported, the scandals, the self-righteous extremists, in fact the things farthest from the norm; and that's just what happens to science in the news, too. The scientists who get the ink are too often the ones with the way-out theories. They bring drama, excitement, a story to the little glass screen.

Some of us do try to read, to educate ourselves, beyond the level of pop journalism and Sunday school classes. There has been a recent glut of popularized books on modern physics. Some, like the *Tao of Physics* or *The Dancing Wu-Li Masters,* try to connect physics with eastern mysticism in a way that leaves both scientists and eastern mystics scratching their heads. A flock of more recent books are by prominent active scientists; they have catchy titles—*The God Particle, The Physics of Immortality*—but too often they present glib expositions whose highest aim is either to fool you into thinking you can understand modern physics in one sitting, or to warn you that it's too hard for little old you—only we wizards, we omniscient scientists, are worthy of grasping the secret mysteries of the quantum quark.

Just as offensive, to me, are books that try to twist twentieth-century physics into a shape that appears to support—surprise!—the nineteenth-century religious Fundamentalism of its authors. They do neither science nor theology any favors. Any philosophy based on twentieth-century physics will surely have its underpinnings knocked away by twenty-first-century physics. And debater's tricks are no substitute for an honest, humble, approach to the truth.

What's worse, for every serious book of science in a bookstore, there's a whole shelf of astrology and UFO nonsense also promising to give you the "secret knowledge" of the universe. In religion, we call this lust for secret knowledge "gnosticism." Science has its gnostics, too. Indeed, the New Age is the place today where bad religion meets bad science.

But in the popular culture, the place where most of us learn about science or religion—especially traditions or fields different from our own experience—are in stories. All modern fiction makes assumptions about science and religion. A good mystery, for instance, can depend on the physical possibility of certain events (science) and the ethics of the characters involved (religion). Science fiction is very explicit in making these concepts central to its story.

Stories, myths, and tales have always made ideas a part of popular culture. Great religious figures teach us with parables. Fables and fairy tales are the way we teach our children about life. And even the ancient Greek myths, it has been argued, might have been deliberate devices for organizing and transmitting information about the natural world to nonscientific people.

Once an idea gets turned into a story, people pay attention long enough to listen. They feel comfortable evaluating it, by comparing the story against their own lives. And they remember it. The images from Dante are much more vivid than the arguments of Aquinas.

So what do our stories tell us about science and religion? One message all too present is that both are to be feared, each in its own way. In the movies, all preachers are power-hungry, money-driven hypocrites; all scientists are mad. They're both caricatured by wild hair and a fanatical gleam in the eye.

Common misreadings of the Bible reinforce a fear of science, or knowledge. Though Adam's sin was pride (not sex!), a fast misreading of his story would refer to him partaking of the fruit of the tree of knowledge. Never mind that it was actually the knowledge of good and evil, and that the Church actively supports schools and scholarship; the implication (especially among the less sophisticated) is that too much knowledge itself is sinful.

The technological achievement of the Tower of Babel brought its makers to no good end. Though the sin being punished was again pride, not tower building, it would be easy to draw a mistaken connection between pride, technology, and sin.

Likewise, listen to God speaking in the book of Job:

Where were you when I laid the foundation of the earth? Tell me, if you have understanding! Who determined its measurements—surely you know!—or stretched the line upon it? On what were its bases sunk, or who laid its cornerstone, when the morning stars sang together, and all the sons of God shouted for joy?

Have you commanded the morning since your days began, and caused the dawn to know its place? Have you entered into the springs of the sea, or walked in the recesses of the deep? Have the gates of death been revealed to you, or have you seen the gates of deep darkness? Have you comprehended the expanse of the earth? Declare if you know all this!

The writer of Job was merely reflecting a common, and understandable, reaction to the awfulness of nature. (Just consider the original meaning of the word "awful.") There's something about the hugeness of the universe, and its terrible power, that can make you very hesitant to try to understand it . . . to suspect that these are things man was not meant to know—quoting a famous line from a truly bad 1950s science fiction movie (*Donovan's Brain*). At first blush, at least, that's what God in the Book of Job is telling us here. To know too much is morally dangerous. Know your place, puny human!

(Of course, a deeper reading of Job can draw the opposite conclusion; that God is actually inviting Job to learn all these mysteries. But that's one of those interpretations you have to look for, in order to find.)

This fear of science and fear of technology (the two are usually confused in the popular mind) is only reenforced by the twentieth century's legacy of atomic bombs and eco-disasters. The arrogance of those who speak in public for science (usually themselves science-fundamentalists) only makes matters worse.

Religion is similarly vilified in popular stories, particularly in science fiction, where it is often portrayed as a tool of fearful mobs out to suppress science. I find this thread even in some of the best science fiction, some of my favorite stories. Isaac Asimov's classic story *Nightfall* is one chilling example; a modern variant can be found in the film *Contact*.

In Castel Gandolfo during the summer of 1995, I overheard our 75-year-old Italian rector, Father Maffeo, struggling on the telephone with an American whose English was beyond his ability to comprehend. Finally, he said, "Please, perhaps you can just send us a fax . . ." A few hours later, the fax arrived, and he showed it to me. It was from the Hollywood production company of the movie *Contact*. They described the plot of their film, based on the novel by Carl Sagan about the first contact between Earth and other intelligence in space. They mentioned that the movie planned to have a scene involving the Vatican Observatory, and they wanted to know . . . well, guess. Was it, what our reaction to extraterrestrial contact would be? No. Who we were and what sort of research we did? No. They only wanted photographs of our hallways, so that they could build realistic-looking sets.

We laughed, and shrugged, and sent them the photographs. We certainly didn't expect to be honestly portrayed—we know Hollywood—but we figured it would probably be good for a laugh.

A month later, another fax arrived. "We are looking for Verses of specific Scripture in the bible that deals with or talks about 'doomesday', the the future of the world or the world coming to an end. Would you happed to know what section of the bible would focus on this topic or do you know specific versus that refer to or mention this." [I'm quoting their spelling and punctuation as written.]

This was, too much, even for me. Not knowing whether to bite my tongue, or simply hold it in cheek, I replied: "There are several biblical passages that sound 'apocalyptic'—try *The Book of the Apocalypse.*" I then went on to point out that John's Revelation, also known as the Apocalypse, was in fact a stylistic history of the first-century Roman persecutions and not actually about the end of the world. Indeed, what the *Contact* people were looking for probably wasn't in the Bible.

(I ran into Carl Sagan himself that fall, at a planetary sciences conference, and told him this story. I thought the bit about "try the Book of the Apocalypse" would raise a smile. It didn't. He merely sighed, and said, "That scene's no longer in the film.")

So there's the first element in the science-religion split. It's fear . . . fear of science and the abuses that can come from its power (a fear all too justifiable, unfortunately). And its counterpoint is the fear that scientists have of anyone outside themselves passing judgment on what should or should not be done . . . fear of the fearful. To the extent that each side misunderstands what the other side is about, and what the other side is afraid of, each fear has fertile room to grow. If scientists and the religious allow these fears to keep them apart, then both groups can only lose.

Another cause for perceiving a science-religion rift is a confusion in the popular culture over the overlapping roles of religion and science.

Worshipping God engages us in something bigger than ourselves. Religion tries to describe, in terms we can only grasp intuitively, things that are beyond our intuition. Where else in our lives do we attempt to deal with the ineffable, to describe the indescribable, to make sense out of a universe that at first glance can seem chaotic? Well . . . science.

Look at the parallels. Religion can be broken into various components—the liturgical practices, where we encounter God, like an observer encounters nature; the theology, that develops a theory of how God relates to us humans; and the moral laws that translate those theories into solving practical how-are-we-to-live-our-lives kinds of problems—sort of like engineering.

When we try to understand God, we're trying to describe the indescribable. We recognize that all our descriptions, ultimately, are inadequate. But we eventually develop an instinct for how far we can push a particular image of God and make it useful, and when we have to abandon that image. These instincts are exactly the same as what we use to understand the universe through science. Science is also a set of human-made descriptions of how an ineffable universe behaves.

It's because of these parallels that science and religion can easily be seen as rivals. They look like two separate entities vying to do the same job.

But religion plays a lot of roles in our popular culture. Religion is the ultimate arbiter of right and wrong: the conscience of society. Whom do we trust to teach our children morality? The President? Congress? Hollywood? Newspapers? The marketplace of ideas? Ourselves as parents? Or should we look to the science of psychology to give us the rules that will turn guilt into mere guilt feelings, and free us from sin (or codependence, anyway)?

Birth, marriage, death, all of them call for a priest or a rabbi, or other religious authority. Most importantly, religion is the activity that deals with ultimate questions. Where do we come from? Where are we going? The priest or minister or rabbi is the person many people go to first when they have these ultimate questions. Where can we find satisfaction for our search for the transcendent? In patriotism? Political parties? Football teams? Everyone has a religion, whether they admit it or not. For some it's Catholicism; for others, Vegetarianism or Elvis or Linux/Macintosh/Windows.

Science can make no claim to the roles that religion plays in our lives. Although science, especially astronomy, has often been called upon to answer the ultimate questions, virtually all astronomers of my acquaintance, believers or not, feel really uncomfortable filling that role. Science is great as science, but it makes a lousy religion. It deliberately refuses to look at the transcendent, for the very good reason that it knows its tools can't handle it.

Furthermore, science keeps changing. Even though real religion may change the words it uses to try to convey its big ideas, the core points that the writers of Genesis were trying to get across 3000 years ago are still valid. Show me a science book that won't look pretty silly 3000 years from now.

Along with the mutual fear that exists between science and religion, and the confusion of roles in the popular culture, there's a third source of the perceived science-religion conflict. It's a fundamental misconception of how both science and religion work.

In the popular imagination, scientists all reflect the ideal—or stereotype—of the logical positivists: cold, methodical, and above all, rational. By contrast, religious characters in books, movies, and television shows are almost always presented as, literally, men of faith: those who believe by instinct, good or bad, but not by proof. See the emotionless Spock versus the touchy-feely Captain Kirk on *Star Trek,* and Spock's spiritual descendants (Data, et al.) in the subsequent shows. Science, we are told, is based on cold, heartless logic; religion, on emotion-filled faith.

But Christianity does not start with faith. It starts with experience. Faith is our reaction to that experience.

Likewise, most scientists know that science is neither so rational, nor so black and white, as the science fiction author would believe.

Yes, we accept science for the very pragmatic reason that "it works." It gives consistent, repeatable, and adequate explanations for natural phenomena. But that alone is not enough. Physics only "works," in the judgment of the physicist, if it not only explains what we observe, but also only if it can predict what we will observe under future circumstances and—most critically—only if it does so in a way that is consistent with all the other laws, in a way that somehow echoes the flavor of those laws, in a manner that the mathematicians call "elegant."

But who's the arbiter of elegance? Following William of Occam, the scientist prefers the simplest explanation that explains all the facts.

But how you judge what's "simple" is as subjective as judging what's "elegant."

Through it all, actually all we hope is that our physical descriptions are a faithful evocation of some ineffable truth—like a good painting, or a poem. Or a prayer.

Ultimately, science does not begin with logic or experiment; it starts with *intuition,* the nonrational functioning of the human mind that leads us to perform those experiments or work out that logic in the first place.

One of the most common experiences of science is that a conclusion arrived at through the use of logic and reason—a theory—can later be overturned by experiment. Indeed, that's the way it's supposed to work. If experiments only confirmed our theories, they'd tell us nothing new and we would learn nothing new. We expect (indeed, we live for the day) that our rational chains of thought will be proved incomplete.

But notice what this means. Any scientific conclusion arrived at by reason alone is not something you believe without further question, but rather something about which you momentarily accord a willing suspension of disbelief until it is confirmed or denied by experiment. What we experience when we observe the results of an experiment may be laden with theory but nonetheless it participates to at least some degree in a direct apprehension of truth.

Logic only takes you so far in the real world, because the real world is always more complicated than any logical system.

There are many phenomena of nature that science can predict and even control, but for which no fundamental well-grounded theory yet exists. There are also beautifully elegant theories that as yet have not been experimentally verified. For example, there seems to be some correlation between weather on Earth and the 11-year cycle of the Sun's magnetic field, but we're still working to come up with a mechanism to explain why this connection is logically inevitable. At the other extreme, there are strong logical reasons to assume that comets come from a cloud—the so-called "Oort cloud"—of cometary material 100,000 astronomical units (AU) from the Sun; but no one has ever observed this cloud directly.

Both the solar-terrestrial weather connection and the Oort cloud are examples of scientific work in progress. By contrast, I once heard the University of Maryland physicist, Charles Misner, point out that the truly established theories of science are a body of knowledge he refers to as "archival theories." He notes that all theories fail eventually, which is to say that all theories—all logical constructions—work only for a limited, finite set of conditions. An archival theory is one whose limitations and regions of failure are well known and documented.

For instance, Newtonian physics fails as one approaches the speed of light, but its method of failure is quite well known and understood. Thus one can say with quite good precision just how accurate Newtonian physics should be for any given set of circumstances. Moreover, further developments in Newtonian physics are not anticipated. In this sense, Newtonian physics is complete. A theory is considered completely established only when we know where and how it fails.

Notice what this says about "rational" systems in general, however. *All rational systems fail.* And the only reliable rational systems are the ones whose failures are well—rationally—understood.

But if all rational systems fail, then there must be another route to truth that tells us that they fail. The scientist calls this, "experiment." And experiments involve the intuitive grasp of natural truths.

There's an even more fundamental reason to challenge the reign of logic as the only path to truth. The fact is, all logic is ultimately based on intuition. Consider the infamous syllogism: All men are mortal; Socrates is a man; ergo, Socrates is mortal. How do we know that all men are mortal? How do we know that Socrates is a man? And even allowing for an epistemology that lets us make those first two statements, what in the human mind gives us the certainty to "conclude" that the third statement "follows" from the first two?

Even ignoring the old saw that this syllogism proves "all men are Socrates," consider what happened to a friend of mine, a Peace Corps teacher in Africa. Paul Gigliotti once encountered a group of 11-year-old boys beating a lizard to death. Knowing that lizards helped keep the insect population in control, the teacher tried to stop the boys from killing the animal.

"But it's a snake!" they insisted.

Paul responded, "Do snakes have legs?"

"No," answered the boys.

"Does this animal have legs?" asked Paul.

"Yes."

"Is this a snake?"

"Yes, yes, kill it!" answered all the boys together.

Logic is learned. It is only through much practice that we develop the intuition that allows us to use logical thinking.

A scientist works largely by intuition. Given enough experience, a scientist examining a problem can leap to an intuition as to what the solution "should look like." The proposed solution is subjected to certain obvious tests: assuming the solution can be quantified, a back-of-the-envelope calculation checks to see if the order of magnitude of the numbers match known values; extreme cases are checked to see if they lead to obvious absurdities. Only after a number of these quick and dirty tests are passed, and the scientist has considerable confidence in his/her theory, will the time and effort be spent in attempting to "prove" the theory more rigorously via chains of logical reasoning.

Logic in science acts like a series of stepping-stones. After an expert has leapt across the stream (and scouted out the far bank to see if there's anything worth seeing there), stepping-stones are set in place to allow the nonexpert to follow a chain of trivially easy leaps to the same result. Logic rarely leads to new insights. Rather, its role is to support the intuition after the leap of insight has occurred.

One can hope that by making the intuitive steps small enough, it will be easier for someone else to follow our intuition and it will be easier for us to retrace the steps of our own insight, thus allowing us to check for errors along the way. The smaller the step, the less likely we are to slip. On the other hand, the greater the number of steps, the greater the number of chances we have to slip.

Science is ultimately based on insight, not logic. But it uses logic to explain and test and develop the insights on which it is based.

Religion is not all that different. To say it is based on faith, not logic, is both false and totally misrepresents what we mean by faith.

Explaining faith is like trying to explain a joke, or trying to describe a color to a blind person. You can talk about wavelengths and light, but a color must be experienced to be believed. I think that's why religion is wasted on the young; it's only as you grow older that you have enough experience to be able to say, "Ah! So that's what they were talking about!"

Both faith and science begin with experience intuited axiomatically. Both must then be developed logically.

Certainly religion cannot be "based" on logic. A "proof" of God cannot exist for it would imply a philosophical or logical structure bigger than the thing it's trying to prove, which is a contradiction of our definition of God. But religion takes the intuition of a God acting in our experience, and tests with the most stringent of logic the possible implications of that experience.

Indeed, what could be more illogical than to be an atheist? If you're wrong, as Pascal pointed out, you risk losing everything when you die; while if you're right, what good does it do you?

Of course Pascal's "wager" is a totally unsatisfying reason to believe in God. Why? Because it appears to have no concern as to whether our beliefs are *true* or not. But if you assume—by intuition—that there is a Truth underlying everything; that finding that Truth is important; and that anything less than that Truth would never satisfy; then that very hunger for Truth is itself a demonstration of something transcendent.

And yet that demonstration, strong as it is, is not the whole story.

The religious world view, indeed the Judeo-Christian world view, indeed the very specific Catholic world view, is the one way of looking at the world that is the most complete and consistent with my own experience—both as a scientist and as a human being.

The idea of a creator God, so different from the pagan religions surrounding the writer of Genesis, means that creation itself is based on law, not chaos. Only in such a universe does science stand a chance of succeeding.

And my human experience goes beyond merely the regularity of nature as seen in science. The Incarnation means that this creation has been sanctified by God's presence. Only such a faith can also explain the beauty I experience in understanding that regularity and the love I have for nature and its beauty and its laws.

And only the story of the fall and redemption can explain the loves and trials and shortcomings I experience in my human life, even when I am not busy doing the work of a scientist.

But even that's not the whole story.

The fact that my personal experience of God, in worship and in prayer, is so identical to the experiences of religious people in so many different times and places and cultures, tells me that either there's an underlying truth we are all sharing—like the truth of our experience of the color purple—or else we are all hallucinating in exactly the same manner. Occam's Razor, the prime tool of all scientists, cuts pretty cleanly here.

But even that's not the whole story.

The fact is, I do personally experience God. I have, always, from earliest childhood. (The ability to do that is what some mislabel as "faith"; I'd say faith is our response to that experience.) Be it a gift or a curse—as it seems sometimes!—that experience is something that we have ultimately no control over. When it happens, we can respond to it or deny it. But if it's not there, we can't make it come by force of will.

The science-fundamentalist believes, and the religious funda-mentalist fears, that religion is a fairy tale suitable only for children, and that once you learn science it will leave no more room for reli-gion. But that just doesn't happen.

Some people are tone-deaf. It's not their fault, and I don't criticize them for it. But I might get bent out of shape if a tone-deaf person insisted that my love of music was a hallucination, based on lies my parents taught me.

Or more absurdly, that my love of music would go away once I'd learned the physics of sound waves.

FINDING GOD IN CREATION

CIENCE AND theology both start with intuition, taking flashes of insight and using the structure of logic—steps of axiomatic intuitions—to clarify and communicate them. This method, enshrined today as the "scientific" method, is in fact a direct development of scholastic, medieval theology. It's no surprise that their methods look similar; they share a common ancestry. For that reason, true theology cannot be in conflict with science, because it is itself a branch of science—indeed, the first branch of science.

And there is an even deeper connection between science and religion. Good science is a very religious act. The search for Truth is the same as the search for God. And if you accept that God was the creator of this physical universe, then it immediately follows that studying creation is a way of worshipping the creator.

This is not some new-millennium take on religion. It's an idea at the heart of traditional Christianity, dating from Roman times. And it was a major departure from classical Greek and Roman ideas.

Writing in the early fifth century, St. Augustine relates in his *Confessions* a key moment when, struggling to accept Christianity and challenged by the question of evil in the world, he finally understood that a good God created only a good universe. He suddenly saw that all things that exist must, to some degree, participate in that good; and that evil in creation was the absence of good, not an entity in its own right. This idea was a development far beyond the neoplatonism in which Augustine had been raised, and far different from the Manichean beliefs ("soul is good, body is bad") he had lived with for so many years.

Yet this new idea, that "body" is good, too, was not original to Augustine, either. As he made clear, it was an insight that he learned from Christianity.

To Augustine, Christianity had proclaimed a radical new order to the "hierarchy" of knowledge. The ancient Greeks, especially Aristotle, thought that physics was subservient to metaphysics. The very word "metaphysics" means "beyond physics." And even physics, as they understood it, was not to be confused with mere "techne," the ability to manipulate nature.

It wasn't only the Greeks. The conflict between the "spiritual" and "physical" worlds led the Hindu civilization to reject the physical world; as a result, Hindu mathematics might rival that of the west but its science never developed beyond what they borrowed from the Greeks.

Even in China, the emphasis of Confucius on honorable human behavior separated good humans from a nature that was, at best, neutral. The idea that nature is good, and that understanding nature is a pathway to God, is a sharp break from these other traditions.

This concept can be traced immediately to the Hebrew belief in God as creator of the universe, who states in Genesis that His creation was good. The Psalms are filled with love of nature and its creation. The Moslems, too, developed a quite extensive scientific knowledge as they, too, accept the creator God of Genesis.

However, Christianity took this concept much further. Rather than merely good, creation has been sanctified. The deepest expression of this idea is most obviously found in the doctrine of the Incarnation: God become Man.

How did this idea of a sanctified creation develop? One can find it in the writings of the fourth-century theologian, St. Athanasius, who obviously influenced Augustine. And one can find a ninth-century version of it in the writings of John "the Scot" Eriugena.

Their writings show that the concept of nature as good, and as a pathway to God, was well understood and taught by Christian thinkers over a long period of time. But, by the way these arguments are presented, one can also get an idea of the sort of counterarguments each man was attempting to refute. The counterconcept of nature as evil clearly is just as long-lived. It's an ever-recurring heresy within the Christian culture.

St. Athanasius' brief work, *On the Incarnation,* is perhaps one of the first writings to expound on the theme. He wrote this book in 318, and how it came to be written is an interesting story. He was only 20 years old at the time; he wrote it for a friend who was a recent convert to Christianity. It was not meant to be an exposition of new ideas but rather a concise summary of Christian thought as he understood it. As a result, he naively presents arguments that he has always understood and taken for granted, not knowing that in fact what he is saying had never really been said in quite that fashion ever before. Uninhibited by the weight of trying to fit into what "scholars always say," he wound up saying something quite new.

At that time, Christian teachings had been getting mixed in with traditional Greek and Roman philosophy, and that had led to a number of variations on what we now call "gnostic dualism": the belief that the spiritual ideal was to be achieved by rejecting the physical universe.

"Marcianism" for instance separated God the Father of whom Jesus spoke from the mere "artisan god" who created the universe in Genesis. If the world were essentially evil, as they believed, then it seemed inconceivable that God could be responsible for its creation. And certainly a good God would never be truly incarnated as man, if created man were essentially evil in nature.

This was the issue St. Athanasius addressed head-on. He began his work by examining the root of the need for a Savior. Creation from the beginning was good, he insists. However, humans with their free will had rejected the goodness of nature. This is how he puts it:

> Men thought little of the grace they had received, and turned away from God. They fashioned idols for themselves in place of the truth, and reverenced things-that-are-not, rather than the God-who-is. They were, as St. Paul says, "worshipping the creature rather than the Creator."
>
> Moreover, and much worse, they transferred the honor due to God to material objects such as wood and stone. They worshipped evil spirits as gods, to satisfy their lusts. They sacrificed brute beasts and immolated men, as the just due of these deities, thereby bringing themselves more and more under their insane control.
>
> Magic arts also were taught among them, oracles in sundry places led men astray, and the cause of everything in human life was traced to the stars, as though nothing existed but that which could be seen.

Notice how he develops the theme. Athanasius here first emphasizes that God is greater than nature. The philosophical problem with idolatry is that you're worshipping something merely created, and less than God, an act in response merely to lusts. But notice what he also has to say about astrologers and other types of fortune tellers. To study the "oracles" of nature, be they entrails or the positions of stars, was wrong not because it doesn't work (the modern scientific argument) but because it implies a purely materialistic, deterministic universe; that "nothing existed but that which could be seen."

In all of this rejection of the gross material world, in favor of God, one might think that Athanasius was following a typical gnostic line: physical world bad, spirituality good. But in the section immediately following, Athanasius turns the tables:

> As a safeguard against their neglect of this grace, God provided the works of creation as a means by which the Maker might be known.

And to make sure you don't miss the point, he continues:

> Mortals could look up into the immensity of heaven, and by pondering the harmony of creation come to know its Ruler, the Word of the Father, Whose all-ruling providence makes known the Father to all.

The evil of idolatry comes not merely because it is the worship of a lesser, created realm. It is a perversion of the true purpose for which the created realm was given to humans.

The purpose of the stars is not to give astrologers a way of predicting the future. It is to give all who view them a taste of the grandeur of God.

This is it! This is the new idea. This is where Athanasius, and Christianity, breaks from the dualist views of the gnostics, and from the whole tradition of pagan science before it.

There was, of course, an opposite extreme that Athanasius worried about. By rejecting the gnostic dualism of spirit/good, matter/bad, one might fall instead into the trap of thinking that the spiritual world was irrelevant.

The question that Athanasius dealt with was, "Why did God become man?" If the material world were evil, there'd be no point in redeeming it. If it were sufficiently good, there'd be no need for an Incarnation. He writes to his friend:

> Perhaps you will say, then that creation was enough to teach men about the Father. But . . . creation was there all the time, and yet it did not prevent men from wallowing in error.
>
> It was the role of the Word of God, and His alone whose ordering of the universe reveals the Father, to renew the same teaching.
>
> But how was He to do it? By the same means as before, perhaps you will say, that is, through the works of creation. But this was proven insufficient. Men had neglected to consider the heavens before, and now they were looking in the opposite direction.
>
> For that reason, in a way altogether natural and fitting, desiring to do good to men, He dwells as Man, taking to Himself a body like the rest. And through His actions, done in that body, as it were on their own level, He teaches those who would not learn by other means to know Himself, the Word of God, and through Him the Father.

The Incarnation was necessary not because of any fault of nature, but because of the fault of men. Still, through it all, creation itself deserved awe, because it proclaimed the greatness of God.

Then he develops a new argument in favor of creation and its study. Indeed, he points out, only creation can proclaim God to us, the created, because without creation there is literally no "thing" for us creatures to encounter. If we are to sense God, God must be sense-able. Thus, it is through creation, and only through creation, that God can communicate with us.

> Human and human-minded as men were, therefore, to whichever side they looked in the sensible world they found themselves taught the truth. Were they awe-stricken by creation? They beheld it confessing Christ as Lord.

But that being the case, the expression of God through nature has an interesting effect on nature itself. And here he comes with his final, stunning insight.

> Invisible and imperceptible as in Himself He is, the Incarnate Redeemer became visible through His works and revealed Himself as the Word of the Father, the Ruler and King of the whole creation. Being the Word, so far from being Himself contained by anything, He actually contained all things Himself. In creation He is present everywhere, yet is distinct in being from it.

(This last phrase is important, because Athanasius rejects a sort of new-age pantheism; he's careful to never confuse the supernatural, God, with the merely natural that is His creation.)

And then comes the stunner:

> Just as the Sun is not defiled by the contact of its rays with earthly objects, but rather enlightens and purifies them, so He Who made the Sun is not defiled by being made known in a body, but rather the body is cleansed and quickened by His indwelling.

Not only is God and the word of God made manifest in creation—a fact that was true from the moment of creation itself. But the incarnation of the word has transformed the creation itself.

Creation is different from how it would have been if there had been no Incarnation. The Body is "cleansed and quickened."

It is a theme that Athanasius returns to at the end of his book. There, he is answering the objections of the Gentiles that creation is not worthy of containing God:

> Perhaps, because humanity is a thing created and brought into being out of nonexistence, some people regard the manifestation of the Savior in our nature as "unfitting." If so, it is high time that they spurned Him from creation too; for it, too, has been brought out of non-being into being by the Word. But if, on the other hand, it is fitting for the Word to be present in creation even though it is a thing that has been made, then it is likewise fitting for Him to be in man. Man is a part of the creation, as I said before; and the reasoning that applies to the one applies to the other.
>
> Nothing in creation had erred from the path of God's purpose for it, save only man. Sun, moon, heaven, stars, water, air, none of these had swerved from their order, but, knowing the Word as their Maker and their King, remained as they were made.

Notice what gets slipped into this argument, almost without thinking: humankind is a part of creation. The whole of his argument centers on this fact; having established that creation can contain God, and show us the path to God, Athanasius now uses the statement that man is a part of creation to argue that the Incarnation is reasonable, that God can be present in the person of the man Jesus.

But this identification of humankind and nature, recognizing humanity as a part of nature, is in fact a revolutionary idea. Aristotle refers to man as a rational animal, but clearly it's the rational part that is of interest to him. Athanasius here is refusing to forget the animal part. Probably only a young person could have said such a thing; anyone older, wiser, and more in tune with philosophy would never make such a "mistake."

The implications are far-reaching. The study of "techne" and the study of nature is as worthy an occupation for a philosopher as the study of humanity itself. But even more, if human beings are a part of nature, then human life, even the human psyche, may all possibly be subject to the arts, the "techne," the same manipulation of the material world that can be applied to building houses or growing crops. One cures disease, even diseases of the soul, by technique, not magic.

That's what G. K. Chesterton meant when, writing his *Short History of England* nearly a hundred years ago, he noted that "a mystical materialism marked Christianity from its birth; the very soul of it was a body. Among the stoical philosophies and oriental negations that were its first foes it fought fiercely and particularly for a supernatural freedom to cure concrete maladies by concrete substances."

To appreciate how radical this concept is, merely compare it to the attitudes of the Hindus or the Chinese. Where are their Michael DeBakeys or Thomas Edisons, their Mayo Clinics and MIT's? And all of this results from the Incarnation, says Athanaseus:

> I take up now the point I made before, namely that the Savior did this in order that He might fill all things everywhere with the knowledge of Himself, just as they are already filled with His presence, as the Divine Scripture says: "The whole universe was filled with the knowledge of the Lord."
>
> If a man looks up to heaven, he sees there His ordering . . . again, if a man has been immersed in the element of water and thinks that it is God—as indeed the Egyptians do worship water—he may see its very nature changed by Him and learn that the Lord is Creator of all. And if a man has gone down even to Hades, still he may see the fact of Christ's resurrection. For the Lord touched all parts of creation, and freed and undeceived them all from every deceit.
>
> Thus Man, enclosed on every side by the works of creation, everywhere—in heaven, in Hades, in men and on the earth—beholds the unfolded Godhead of the Word.

It is not just humankind, but the whole of creation, that was transformed and elevated by the existence of Christ.

In *On the Incarnation* Athanaseus explicitly states that creation is good, and that it is a path to lead us to God. He argues against those who assume creation is evil. And he brings forth the insight that by participating personally in His creation, God has elevated the status of nature. By implication, he maintains that the honor and duty of one who knows and loves God is to know and love His creation.

In other words, God calls us to be scientists.

Athanasius wrote as a young man, almost certainly unaware that the arguments he deduced almost as commonplaces from the ideas of his times were so novel or so important. But like most philosophical debates, the real developments occurred not in the stated arguments but in the hidden assumptions that the arguers may not even have been aware that they were making.

Almost all the other philosophers assumed without question that humankind was superior to creation, different from creation in both purpose and destiny. Athanasius, by using the "obvious" fact that humanity is a part of creation, didn't realize how he was changing the ground rules of talking about man or creation.

Did these ideas survive? Were they developed? Were they opposed?

To take another snapshot in time, turn to the writings of John "the Scot" Eriugena (Joannes Scotus Eriugena). Writing in the ninth century, he attempted in his *Perphyseon, On the Division of Nature* to organize the understanding of creation on a theological basis.

His division was based on function and origin. According to him, there is first of all that which creates and is not created, namely, God; second, there is that which creates and is created, which is God's manifestation of Himself through the primordial causes of the visible world. The effects of these causes, that which is created but does not create (in essence, what we today would call nature) are the third division. The final division is that which is neither created nor creative, namely, God as the goal of all (what the twentieth-century German theologian Karl Rahner called the Term of our Transcendence).

In looking at his work, a few differences between Eriugena and Athanasius must be kept in mind.

First, difficult as his times were for Athanasius, Eriugena is writing in intellectually far more trying circumstances. Athanasius' world was one of active intellectual ferment, stirred up by ideas from across the Roman empire, based on a well-established canon of classical knowledge. Eriugena came at the end of 400 years of Dark Ages, with scholarship in hiding against barbarian invasions and Viking raids. For him, access to classical texts was much more constrained, and his opportunity to converse with other scholars was virtually nonexistent.

Because scholarship was in such a precarious state, thinking was understandably much more conservative. Thus, he was hampered by a mind-set that viewed the past, and all books of the past, with an inordinate respect.

And finally, even if all other things had been equal, I suspect Eriugena still wasn't in the same class as Athanasius as a writer or thinker.

There's a specific reason why I make this harsh judgment of John the Scot, and it ties in with the section of his writing that I'm going to talk about.

In discussing the third class of creation, nature, John engaged in a long exegesis of Genesis. He examined each day of creation in light of the best scientific knowledge of his day. It is clear from his citations that he was well aware of the best astronomy of the ancient Greeks. For instance, he quoted correctly the (remarkably accurate) circumference of the Earth derived by Eratosthenes of Alexandria in 225 B.C. However, when he then attempted to explain how Eratosthenes derived this number, he got both the facts of the case and the logic behind them completely muddled. Making matters worse, he then attempted to find the diameter of the Earth from its circumference by dividing it not by π, which was well known by then, but by two!

Likewise, he discussed the arrangement of the Sun and planets: placing the Earth at the center of the universe and the stars on a celestial sphere surrounding the Earth, he then assumed (quoting "the philosophers" without naming any) that the Sun circled the Earth at a distance halfway between the stars and the Earth. So far, this is certainly not too far from the typical Ptolemaic, heliocentric view. But then he derived the positions of the other planets based on their colors:

> The planets that revolve around the Sun change their colors in accordance with the qualities of the regions they are traversing, I mean Jupiter and Mars, Venus and Mercury, which always pursue their orbits around the Sun, as Plato teaches in the *Timaeus* . . .

. . . their orbits around the Sun! It's one of the more frustrating statements in the history of science. Here he was in effect anticipating Tycho Brahe's cosmology by 750 years, an essential step towards the heliocentric view; but he didn't realize it. This view of the solar system should have been revolutionary, but in fact it was generally ignored . . . for the very valid reason that it was based on nothing but a sloppy, incorrect reading of Plato. (If you go read the *Timaeus,* you find Plato actually saying that all the planets revolve around the Earth.)

However, it is not Eriugena the astronomer, with all his failings, that we are interested in here but rather Eriugena's philosophical defense of the fact that he bothers to look at astronomy at all. After finishing his arguments concerning the order and distances of the planets, he wrote:

So much for the philosophical arguments that investigate the cosmic distances. But if these seem to anyone superfluous since they are not ratified or transmitted by the testimonies of Holy Scripture, let him not rebuke us. For neither can he prove that these things are not so, just as we cannot confirm that they are.

And nothing definite is found in the divine Scriptures concerning such measurements of the sizes and distances of the bodies of the world. "For who," asks Ecclesiastes, "has measured the height of heaven and the breadth of the Earth and the depth of the abyss?" which I think we should understand in an allegorical rather than an historical sense. For I would not say that the constitution of this world lies outside the understanding of the rational nature when it was for that nature's sake that it was created.

Yet the Divine Authority not only does not prohibit the investigation of the reasons of things visible and invisible, but even encourages it. For, says the Apostle, "from the creation of the world His invisible things are seen, being understood from the things that have been made." Therefore it is no small step, but a great and indeed profitable one, from the knowledge of the sensibles to the understanding of the intelligibles.

For as through sense we arrive at understanding, so through the creature we return to God. For we ought not like irrational animals look only on the surface of visible things, but also give a rational account of the things that we perceive by the corporeal sense. The eagle sees more clearly the form of the Sun; the wise man sees more clearly its position and motion through places and times.

First, note the implied opposition in the opening paragraph. Eriugena must have encountered those who would demean the study of nature in favor of the study of theology. The lesson of Athanasius had been forgotten, at least in some quarters; or more likely the spirit of exclusion and intolerance between the fields of science and humanities was just as bad in the ninth century as it was in C. P. Snow's twentieth-century experience, as described in his famous commentary on the "Two Cultures." It is all too easy for any discipline to think of itself as superior, and to view with disdain any outsider's attempt to enter it. (Science today is just as bad at that as theology was back then, by the way.)

The fact that Eriugena thought to mix metaphysics with natural science is not in itself particularly unusual. Aristotle's metaphysical principles (such as the existence of an unmoved mover) are to some degree based on the cosmology he worked out in his *Physics*. The difference here is not the mixing, but the motivation. We study science, says John the Scot, not because it is useful, either for building bridges or bringing us closer to God; we study science because God wants us to.

Follow the trend of this argument: First, the absence of a subject from Holy Scripture is not to be taken as an indication that it is something not to be studied. Our knowledge of God is not limited by scripture (a point St. Thomas Aquinas would emphasize 400 years later). Secondly, the knowledge of things that we can know by virtue of God's gift of intelligence is a knowledge that we are thus instructed by God to pursue. "It was for that nature's sake that it was created." To rewrite his convoluted Latin: our rational nature was created for the sake of learning about the constitution of nature. God gave us brains; He expects us to use them.

In this context he quoted Paul's Letter to the Romans, chapter 1, verse 20: "Ever since the creation of the world his invisible nature, namely, his eternal power and deity, has been clearly perceived in the things that have been made." It's the same passage of Romans that Athanasius used. That is why we are allowed, encouraged, indeed commanded by God to employ that rational nature, and explore the constitution of nature. "Divine Authority not only does not prohibit the investigation of the logic behind things visible and invisible, but even encourages it."

Regardless of what we now think of his physics, or his metaphysics, this lesson of Eriugena is one that deserves to be remembered today. In the post-Galileo atmosphere, it is common for both scientists and theologians to draw strict immutable boundaries between their fields. The fact that so much of our scientific knowledge, like that of classical physics, has been seen to be incomplete has contributed to this division; who wants to base a philosophy on a scientific view that might be overturned tomorrow? But it is important, Eriugena was saying, to remember that our knowledge of God does grow with our knowledge of His creation.

Our theology has grown enormously, in depth and breadth, thanks to the scientific revolution; and our science owes its existence to medieval theology . . . points not to be forgotten, even if scientists and theologians are both embarrassed by these facts. Our theology prepared science to accept the seeming contradictions of quantum theory, for instance; just because something doesn't seem to make sense, is no proof that it must be false. Likewise we know now that our science can be incomplete and fallible, yet still worth studying and pursuing; this is a valuable attitude for theology to remember, as well.

This mixture of science and theology was promoted by St. Athanasius, who urged believers to look toward creation, not away from it; to value the awe with which we behold the stars. It was insisted upon by Eriugena, who saw in human rational capacity a religious mandate to learn about creation by rational means. It is founded on Scripture as basic as Paul's Letter to the Romans.

The desire for truth and understanding, including understanding the truth of the natural world, was given to us by God in order to lead us to God. It is the desire for God. It is why I am a scientist; it is why the Vatican supports me.

PART THREE

ONCE IN A
LIFETIME

HOLES IN THE SAND

O WHO am I, that I
should have gotten this great job?

I am an astronomer, a teacher, a researcher. An American, a baby-
boomer born in Detroit, Michigan, of Italian and Irish ancestry. A
Catholic.

You know, tomorrow, I could lose my job. Tomorrow, I could
learn that some new experiment had overthrown every bit of science
I ever thought I knew. Tomorrow, I could discover that the folks I call
"mom and dad" are really not my true parents, or my country could be
conquered and my citizenship could be lost. But I would still be the
same person. It's my Catholicism that is fundamental, the cornerstone
of my life. It is like a rock in a river holding fast against the currents;
and against this rock I measure my progress, all that I have done and
all I wish to do. It is my axiom from which everything else is deduced.

Once, when I was in high school, I was talking to a friend who confessed that she no longer believed in the Catholic faith. More than anything, I was puzzled. It was like not believing that the Sun would rise in the morning.

"Don't you understand it?" she said. "I was always the good little girl. I still go to communion to set an example for my younger brothers and sisters. But I don't believe in God. Can't you understand what it's like not to believe anymore?"

This was 1969; there were a lot of "revolutionary" thoughts going around, and I was still getting used to the idea that you could disagree with the government and still love your country (and be a good Catholic). But to not believe in God? Sure, I'd heard of atheism, but the concept that I could be an atheist had never occurred to me.

So I tried to imagine what it would be like to live in a world without God. It was like standing at the edge of a terrifying, gaping black pit; I felt a sudden attack of vertigo. I didn't *want* to not believe.

"What?" said a voice inside me. "You're afraid? It's only your fear of the unknown that keeps you a Catholic? Then you don't really believe, either! You're just too scared to give up your comfortable little world! Why, you intellectually dishonest coward!"

And I had the sinking feeling that the voice was speaking the truth.

"But," I asked that voice timidly, "why should I not believe? What's the point of not believing?"

The voice was silent.

A little more bravely, I went on, "Without God, who's there to care that I'm a chicken? What difference would it matter if I'm intellectually dishonest? The fact that it does matter, proves that there's more to the world than just materialism.

"And the fact remains, I don't want to not believe. And you will never, ever, be able to give me a good reason to change my mind."

All this went on in the flash of a few seconds. All my friend saw was my puzzled look. I couldn't figure out how to answer her. I never did.

I have been a rational, logical, convinced Catholic since I can first remember.

Being the youngest in my family, with few neighbors my age to play with, as a kid I was given to long bouts of introspection. During the summers, which we spent on the shores of Lake Huron, I would spend hours digging holes in the sand and letting the lake in. I remember once stopping and wondering about the significance of it all. What did it matter if I dug this little hole? Would it matter any more if I were an adult with a steam shovel, digging a bigger hole? Compared to the lake (and Lake Huron is hundreds of miles wide, a wild, cold, northern inland sea), any hole would pale to insignificance. All human activity, I realized, was insignificant. Only God mattered. Satisfied, I continued to have fun digging in the sand.

The Lake Huron shoreline in a strange way molded my soul. It is not a particularly picturesque area. The land is flat and swampy, the lake cold and rocky. And yet I was surrounded by love and happiness.

I started kindergarten in 1957, the year of Sputnik, and it was clear then that clever little boys like me were supposed to become scientists. I had a chemistry set, a microscope, a dozen electronics kits, a Visible Man and a Visible V-8. I built my own foxhole radio and a room-to-room intercom. (Neither worked.)

I had toy rockets. A telescope. Best of all, my favorite Christmas present: a home planetarium.

And lots and lots of books.

In the fourth grade, I was chosen to lead a group of school children in a demonstration of science education techniques to be held in the city, at the local Jesuit high school, the University of Detroit High. It was the first time I'd heard of that school, much less the Jesuits; but I when heard it was the best, I knew right then I wanted to go to high school there.

I did. But though originally it had been my interest in science that had led me to the Jesuits, my studies now were centered on the Classics, Latin and Greek, along with English Literature and History. The chemistry laboratory in my basement, the electronics kits that never worked, the home planetarium, all were put aside as childish things. But the Jesuits knew what I would come to discover, that science would still be waiting for me when I was ready for it again.

I did a lot of debate and forensics, and a lot of writing. I got very interested in journalism, learned to use a camera and develop film, wound up editor of the school paper. I also took part in various "social action" activities in high school, mostly tutoring neighborhood kids after school or on weekends. The priest who ran this program, knowing that I was a photographer, had me come to downtown Detroit with him to take pictures of the area around the soup kitchen where he had students helping out as volunteers.

The poverty I saw that day hit me like a body blow. I felt guilty, that night, sitting in my comfortable suburban home while visions of the old, run down city tenements still burned in my head. I was not politically active, or particularly liberal, and I didn't interpret what I saw in terms of slogans or causes (though after the Detroit riot in 1967, there were plenty of both around). Instead, it was a more personal fear—what if I had to live in such a place?

The High had annual career days. One career I always signed up to hear about was the priesthood. The idea of becoming a Jesuit was intriguing; I admired them tremendously, and I wanted to be someone who would be admired as much as I admired them.

My first year out of high school I attended Boston College, chosen simply because it was in Boston and it was run by the Jesuits. I had all sorts of different dreams; when it came time to declare a major, I looked for the box that said "all of the above." Finally, I chose History, thinking it could prepare me for journalism or perhaps law school.

Freshman year is universally difficult. Attending in the fall of 1970, in the midst of Vietnam and student strikes, made it all the harder. And a summer working on a small newspaper in Michigan had made me suspect that I really wasn't cut out for journalism . . . it called for an aggressiveness foreign to my nature. I didn't know what I wanted, though at least I had discovered what I didn't want.

Again I fell back on my religion. I attended Mass two or three times a week in the little chapel on campus, and got to know some of the priests. One was Father Healy, who seemed friendly and approachable. So I came to him one day with the idea that I was thinking of becoming a Jesuit. I expected he'd pull out an application form, or something like that.

Instead, he asked me, "Have you prayed about this?"

Huh? I was 18 years old. Who prays?

"Go back to your room," he said, "find a quiet moment, and ask God if this is the path He wants you to take."

So, I went back to my dorm room, closed the door, and sat down on the floor. I stared at the ceiling. "All right, God," I said, "I'm supposed to ask you if I should be a priest. I mean, everybody knows the Church is desperate for priests, so I know what the answer is, but Father Healy said I should ask, so . . ."

Nothing happened.

I stared at the ceiling some more, feeling really stupid. I hoped my roommate wouldn't show up and ask me what the heck I was doing.

Still nothing happened.

While I was waiting for the voice from the ceiling, I started to think about a few things. You know, my reasons for wanting to be a priest included some pretty weak motives—I was an unhappy freshman; I wanted to get away from a college dorm I didn't like; I wanted prestige and respect; I wanted people to admire me.

I thought about the job that a priest has to do. Forget about the religious side for a moment; what is a priest's day-to-day all about? It's about dealing with people, especially helping people in trouble, especially people like the fellow students in my dorm with whom I never got along. It's about working with the poor and disadvantaged, work that I'd always felt particularly inept at when I did volunteer projects in high school. It's about dealing with other people's questions about religion, like the questions my high school friends had that I had never really been able to understand.

It was obvious to me that the talents and abilities God had given me were not the talents and abilities of a priest.

Instead, maybe it was the things that I could do well—like school work—that were the things that I should be concentrating on. If you're short and fat, why try out for the basketball team? I was a nerd. And I was good at it. So why not try out for the nerd team instead? Huh?

It was a terribly surprising revelation; so completely different from what I had thought or expected, so strong and so . . . other . . . that maybe . . .

Maybe this God I was so comfortable with, the God I believed in, passively, because there was no good reason not to . . .

. . . was actually real?

And spoke to me?

And told me things maybe I didn't want to hear.

"I understand, God," I said. "You don't want me to become a Jesuit."

The answer came back. "Not yet."

The last, little, "not yet" was the worst stroke of all. "You mean, maybe later?" I asked in utter confusion.

Of course, this left me in even worse a quandary than before.

In fact, I had been spending my weekends with an old high school friend, Mike Timmreck, attending college up the road from me at MIT. MIT, I discovered, had pinball machines and weekend movies, neat tunnels to explore, and a huge science fiction library.

Most of all, it had lots of stuff I wasn't learning at Boston College: science and technology and cutting-edge research like I'd read about in magazines.

On a whim, I filled out an application form to transfer. Asked to declare a major, I remembered my plastic planetarium and so I looked for the Astronomy department. "What does an astronomer actually do for a living?" I wondered. "Maybe I'll find out." But I couldn't find Astronomy on the list, just "Earth and Planetary Science." I checked it . . . not realizing that it really meant Geology, with a geology-of-other-planets option.

In mid-July, 1971, the shock of my life occurred. I was accepted.

My first year at MIT, I struggled mightily with physics, and it nearly did me in. The terms and phrases in the books just sounded like gibberish, without meaning, and the homework problems were impossible to solve. Because I entered as a sophomore, I had to catch up by taking an intensive physics class that crammed a semester's work into the January break between semesters. For 3 weeks I lived and breathed physics. And one day, something snapped in my head; I gave an answer to a tutor's question, and he looked at me with surprise. "That's right," he said. "How did you know that?"

"I just looked at the units, and I got tired of trying to understand it the way the book wanted me to, but instead it just seemed like it had to be this way, and . . ." And what had happened was, that suddenly I could understand physics. And all those gibberish phrases in the book not only made sense; suddenly they seemed like the most clear and concise and obvious way of putting things.

But the reason I was so surprised, was that this wasn't the first time I'd had such an experience. While I was still at Boston College, my mother had gone into the hospital for an operation. And at first I was terrified for her, but then I was "calmed by the grace of God." At that same moment, I felt myself part of a larger union of people, my mom and my family and all the other people in the world going in for operations, and everyone who'd ever lived or ever would live. And I said to myself, "so this is what they mean by the Mystical Body of Christ. What a perfect way to describe it."

Here it had happened again. Old words about religion had, with experience, meant something real. Now old words about physics finally took on meaning, too. And so, at MIT, I started a game with myself that I've played ever since: drawing parallels between religion and physics. For instance . . .

"The Bible is like my Physics text. They're both about the same size. They both contain a way of dealing with the universe that's withstood the test of time. They both teach by showing you worked-out examples. And they're both pretty useless, if you don't understand how to use them. (Only, the Bible doesn't have the answers in the back of the book.)

"It may be possible to 'find God' without an organized religion; but you'd have about as much hope of getting it right, as you would from trying to derive all of modern physics from scratch on your own.

"Both physics and religion ask you to suspend your disbelief and take, on faith, some pretty unlikely propositions, things that seem counterintuitive. It's only by using these unlikely propositions to solve problems, living with them, testing them by experiment, that you can really fully understand them, and see just under what circumstances they are valid. Experiment is the test of the theory, says the physicist . . . 'by their fruit you shall know them,' says the New Testament.

"Truth does exist, but it's never fully comprehensible. And if you see a contradiction between two things you know must be true, then rather than throwing out one or the other, you have to realize that this is an opportunity to advance, and to learn something new about both things."

I remember discussing with someone the mystery of the divinity of Jesus, and whether this particular unlikely proposition was really necessary. I remember realizing, and saying out loud, that Jesus being God was an essential part of my faith.

"If Jesus were just a very good man," I said, "I'd have no reason to follow his religion. I'm a good man, too—and I guess, in my egotistical way, I'd be inclined to believe that I'm as smart as anyone else, and I could come up with a religion as good as any other human being's. It's the fact that it is God Himself saying these things that makes me stop and listen.

"And it's precisely because my religion has mysteries that I know it has a ghost of a chance of being true. Anything that makes complete sense at first glance can't challenge you, can't possibly teach you anything new, and can't possibly be completely true."

Then someone else recalled a theologian's work contrasting the death of Jesus with the death of Socrates. Where Socrates, who believed in the Greek concept of the soul, calmly drank poison, Jesus—God Himself—sweat blood at the thought of dying. Human life should not be given up calmly or lightly; rather, human life and the things we do in our life really do matter, on a cosmic scale. The little boy's hole in the sand is, somehow, as important as the whole lake.

At MIT I learned a broader tolerance and appreciation of people whose lives were alien to mine. The dorm I lived in, Bexley Hall, had earned its reputation as the "drug dorm" at MIT. Although I was never tempted that way—I value my brain too much to monkey around with it—I learned I could still respect and learn things from people whom I disagreed with. I learned how to fit my parochial views of religion into a larger world.

I was a longhaired Bexleyite, and didn't make an overt thing about my religion, so my friends were often surprised to learn that I went to church on Sundays. I became something of a curiosity, someone who could talk about religion without being uptight about it.

One fellow longhair, a guy I met in a humanities class, was completely blown away to learn I had any religious convictions. He took me aside one afternoon to talk about it.

"I was brought up in West Virginia," he said, "a strict Baptist. And I just couldn't handle that stuff."

"Like what?" I asked.

"You know, they said crazy things would happen if I stopped going to church; that it was the end, it'd be straight to hell for me. I'd become a sinner, and my life would be ruined."

"What kind of things did they think would happen?" I asked.

"I don't know, I guess that I'd start drinking, and hang out with 'sinful women', and do drugs . . ."

"Well," I asked, "did you?"

He stopped.

"You can wipe the smirk off your face," I said. "So, how were they so crazy? I mean, they were right, weren't they?"

He gave me a funny look, and changed the subject.

After 4 years in Cambridge, living in run-down dorms and city apartments, I no longer had the same fear of poverty that I'd had in high school. I'd even joined a tutoring program, helping out a local Cambridge kid with his reading and arithmetic. But working with Jay, my fourth grader, I learned several things. First, I saw firsthand that the poverty he lived in was not simply lack of money or good housing. On a day-to-day basis, my home was not any better than his, and I had no more spending money than his mom did. Rather, the difference was in outlook, attitudes, expectations. His family had no wealthy parents to fall back on in an emergency, nor did they have any reasonable hope that they'd ever be any better off than they were.

Second, I learned that spending time with Jay was a wonderful way for me to keep an honest perspective on my own life. My thesis was not the beginning and end of the universe.

Finally, I learned that, in spite of all that Jay could teach me, I wasn't very much help to him. I was not the big brother he needed, the sort of male role model he could identify with or look up to. I was right not trying to be a priest.

I stayed on an extra year at MIT to turn my undergraduate research into a Master's thesis. Finishing up my last year, however, I was faced once again with choices. Was science journalism my heart's desire? Or maybe my future was with the Jesuits now; I remembered that "not yet" I'd gotten. I prayed. I reflected on my mediocre career as a journalist, and my utter failure as a social worker. And the unexpected success of my master's thesis research. It seemed clear which door God was holding open to me. So I went off to study planetary science at the University of Arizona, in Tucson.

Graduate school was my first experience living exclusively among "adults" instead of undergraduates or kids. And I was appalled by how immature, selfish, and destructive adults seemed to be. The posturing, backstabbing, and politicking among people who were supposedly "eminent scientists"; the casual wife-swapping that went on as people treated relationships, and each other, with callous disregard; the greed for power, pleasure, and money that I'd always been warned about but had never seen firsthand; it all appalled me. It wasn't just that people were immoral—by traditional standards, my druggie friends back in Bexley Hall had these people beat cold—but that they seemed so cheap and stupid about it all.

In the spring of 1977, I had a chance to attend a conference in England. I jumped at that chance. I knew hardly anyone in England; but a friend of a friend set me up with a place to stay outside of London. So I stayed for 2 weeks with a young family, total strangers to me, who accepted me with open arms. I was utterly bowled over by their hospitality. Their love and their goodness was a clear sign to me of God's presence.

But the irony was that they turned out to be devout Baptists—members of a religion I had shown little tolerance for in my life. Certainly they were not perfect . . . there were occasional moments where they showed their equal suspicion of Catholicism. But their warm acceptance of me into their home was the honest, spontaneous action of good hearts in touch with the Holy Spirit.

Indeed, they could show an amusing tolerance even for the points where we disagreed. When I confessed that my excuse for being in England was a conference on the origin of the solar system, they laughingly referred me to Genesis. They told me, "Don't worry . . . you'll learn better, some day."

The love and fulfillment that these good people found in their faith represented a new challenge for me to understand. Were they right? Was God really speaking more clearly to them than to me? By their actions, it certainly seemed so.

But did this mean that their whole fundamentalist view of the world was correct? When faced with a conflict between religion and science, which side would I come down on?

Well, I had already realized that God is supernatural, above nature, and so it would be impossible for any natural argument or experiment to "prove" or "disprove" Him. So certainly, just because the overwhelming weight of scientific evidence contradicts the fundamentalists' view, that cannot by itself prove the veracity of science over the Bible when it comes to questions like origin of the universe.

So I had to ask myself: why did I believe in science? God could have created the world in 7 days. Yet I was convinced that, almost certainly, He didn't. But why was I so convinced? Because it just didn't sound like His way of doing things.

The God who was my friend, whom I'd known all my life, was not the sort of person who'd create a universe in such an inelegant manner. Nor would He leave behind all sorts of nasty "clues" designed to trap scientists into thinking it had been done differently.

Indeed, the best and most wonderful thing about being a scientist was the chance to see God's creation, up close, firsthand, to delight in His cleverness and elegance and to get to know all the better the person who'd done the creating. Just as a writer's personality and background manifests itself in his or her work, the same is true of God and God's creation.

God is a creator who sets up simple rules, and then follows those rules to make a thing of complex beauty. God's universe is "self-similar," ever complicated but based on the same simple pattern that reveals itself, over and over again, everywhere you look. God is a creator whose universe can be appreciated on an infinite number of levels—not only is a sunset beautiful, but so are the Maxwell equations that describe how the light is transmitted from the Sun to us. And God gave us the brains to be scientists precisely so we could share in His delight.

So by doing good, honest science I was not falling into some diabolical trap. Rather, by doing good science, I was worshipping God.

St. Augustine tells about walking along the seashore, pondering a theological mystery, when he encountered a small boy digging a hole in the sand. Comparing the hole to the size of the sea, he realized that trying to fit the mystery of God into his tiny brain was like trying to fit the sea into that hole.

But I am no Augustine. I'm the kid digging in the beach. I could see my little hole as a homage to the much larger sea it imitates. But mostly I see it as having fun.

It's the same release.

CALL AND RESPONSE

FTER COMPLETING
my Ph.D. at Arizona, I found myself back on the East Coast, working
as a researcher and lecturer at my alma mater, MIT. This was Big Science. This was the major leagues . . . and even if my role was not much
more than utility infielder, I was in The Show.

But into my third year at MIT, my work was not going well. A
string of brief romances all turned sour. As the last year of my post-
doctoral position in Cambridge was drawing to a close, I turned 30 and
felt suddenly like my youth and promise were slipping away from me.

Finally, one day while staring out my window at MIT onto the
Charles River, 10 stories below me, I had to face the killer question:
Why was I wasting my time modeling the moons of Jupiter, when
there were people starving in the world?

I realized that, in many ways, I was in an enviable position. I had
no debts or family commitments. I was in good health. I had some

money in the bank, and the skills to earn more if I wanted to. I could do just about anything I wanted. But what did I want?

My postdoctoral research had been stymied by petty jealousies that developed into a bitter feud with a powerful group of planetary scientists from the southwest. I hated the conflict; the stress made me physically ill. It was no longer fun for me to be a part of my field of science.

Furthermore, I felt pressured to publish, and I had started to produce papers that were clearly not good work. When the better journals decided not to publish these inferior papers, I felt depressed for having done such poor science.

I realized that being a scientist was not on my list of things I wanted anymore. Was it time to give up research?

And then the chance of a lifetime appeared before me. This was 1982, and IBM was rumored to be about to introduce a Personal Computer, small enough to sit right on your desktop! And a guy from my dorm at MIT had invented the first piece of big-time business software: *Visicalc,* the first "spreadsheet" program. His company was just up the street in Cambridge. Other friends of mine worked there, and they had a spot for me. I was interviewed. I was offered a position at a salary nearly double my original postdoctoral salary. I would be employee number 51 of the first company to build the "killer-app" that would rake in billions of dollars over the next 10 years.

And just about this time I met a young woman . . . bright, attractive, fun. A librarian—that meant she must be together and reliable and love books to boot. What more could I be looking for?

Walking home from MIT one blustery winter evening, I stood alone halfway across the Harvard Bridge, and saw a vision of my future dancing on the ice of the Charles River before me. It involved a wife, 2.4 kids, a dog and a cat, and a house in Wellesley with a Volvo station wagon parked out front.

It was so close I could smell it, taste it, touch it. My heart was pounding. In a daze, I walked back to my South End apartment. Hand shaking, head spinning, I picked up the telephone while scrambling through the phone book to find the number I needed.

"Hello?" I asked. I stopped to catch my breath. "Uh, yes?" asked the stranger at the other end. "Can we help you?"

"Umm . . . ummm . . . umm . . ." I stuttered. I swallowed hard. "Uh, maybe. Tell me . . . would you guys have any room for a burned-out planetary astronomer, there in the Peace Corps?"

My sister had been in the Peace Corps, back in the 1960s. And when she was in Africa I'd been terrified to think of being alone like her in some jungle overseas. Now, that seemed like just the right move.

By joining the Peace Corps, I could travel. I could teach. I could maybe even do some good for starving people in the world. And at the very least, I could put off for a couple of years the yuppie fate threatening to swallow me, like it had swallowed so many of my old college friends.

Besides, it turned out that the librarian wasn't interested in me, anyway.

I was embarrassed to mention it at MIT, but when I finally announced my Peace Corps plans my friends were surprisingly supportive. Even my boss, Sean Solomon (one of the superstars of geophysics), nodded his approval. My friend Dan Davis added one bit of advice: "Bring a small telescope with you."

I talked to my sister about it, of course. "They'll be sure to take you, with your degrees," she reassured me. "You'll probably wind up in the capital city of some nice country, teaching at the University. You'll have a modern apartment, with running water even, and all the other volunteers will wind up sleeping on your floor when they come into town."

"No way," I said. "I want the real thing!"

But she tempered my send-me-in-coach ambitions. As she pointed out, it took a real attitude of self-sacrifice to go in with no fixed agenda. Just go wherever they sent you, do whatever they asked . . . no matter how hard. Or how easy.

Finally the letter arrived. I would be teaching high school science in a "Harambee" school, the kind of volunteer-run poverty-stricken place with no windows in the windows and no black on the blackboards, in a remote upcountry village of Kenya. Africa!

I trained with 80 other volunteers, most of them fresh out of college. The training itself was an intense shock . . . giving up my beautiful apartment and all my possessions, being out of telephone touch with my family and friends, living in very close quarters with some very bright but very young volunteers, and subjected to a rigid schedule set by someone other than myself.

To be honest, however, it felt wonderful. To give up all my possessions meant I didn't have to worry about losing them anymore! A letter, a tangible gift that could be read over and over, brought far more satisfaction than a telephone call. The young volunteers made me appreciate how much I had gained just by having 10 more years of experience in life . . . it wasn't until I'd left school that I'd had time to learn how to direct a play, sing in a choral group, fix a bicycle. I was no longer afraid of growing old—I was delighted.

I learned how to survive on terrible food. I learned how to speak, and live, in a foreign language. I learned how to wait.

My first day of training, I was promoted out of the Harambee school track into the ranks of those teachers headed to a regular high school. My last day of training, I was assigned a step further up, to an elite "national" school, the Starehe Boys' Centre, a special orphanage in the capital city run by important government officials. Three months after that, they pulled me out of there to move me to the University of Nairobi.

I wound up living in an apartment that was very comfortable by Peace Corps standards. I had electricity and running hot and cold water (when they worked). And I never lacked for houseguests, whenever volunteers arrived into Nairobi to do business with the Peace Corps administration or the government.

I spent most of my time teaching graduate students in physics. Greatest irony of all, I directed graduate students in astronomical research projects: just like the science I'd abandoned back at MIT.

Many Africans were indeed starving in 1984, a year of terrible drought in east Africa. But from my vantage point I could now see that a technologically advanced society was the only kind of society capable of feeding its people with any reliability. And that demanded a technologically literate populace. My students at the University would go on to teach at the Kenya Science Teacher's College; their students would be the high school teachers who would train the high school students who would go on to become the army of technically literate people, from auto mechanics to telephone repair, that a modern society needs to survive. And if my astronomical doodlings made physics exciting and fun, the electrical power grid in the country might be a little more dependable at some future date. So that's why we'd spend our time in a country of starving people, doing astronomy. Right? But something else was going on.

Poverty, disease, and death were commonplace. Life was fragile— and real. God was close to the surface in Kenya. By contrast, in America God had been pushed far away by our "painless" society of insurance and lawyers and miracle drugs.

During training, I spent a week living in a remote shamba with a family where the older generation spoke no English, whose home was a collection of mud huts, who drew their water by hand from a shallow well, and who lived day to day from the food they grew themselves. While the older folks kept the farm going, the eldest son commuted every day into the village where he ran a computer as a teller at Barclay's Bank. The family welcomed me as a special friend, because I was a fellow Catholic.

I was surprised how packed the churches were on Sunday. With a theology that can be obtuse, a liturgy full of ceremony that is stuffed with esoteric symbolism, and sermons given by mission priests whose English or Swahili was often unintelligible, what could these people possibly be getting out of the Mass? Obviously they saw something I was missing. Certainly, the Old Testament stories had an immediacy for people who measured their wealth, like the patriarchs, in sheep, goats, and wives.

To keep in touch with the "real Peace Corps" that I had been denied, and to take advantage of the training I'd gotten, I had made it a point to visit a different volunteer friend upcountry nearly every weekend. Their students got to try out my little telescope on nearby things, trees and houses, to see how it worked; and I'd give a little talk about astronomy. Then, weather permitting, at night we could go out to look at the stars.

Not only the students would line up, so would their teachers, and their parents, and the old men who worked as guards at the school.

One such old man turned to me after viewing Jupiter, with a rapt look and a wide, toothless smile.

"What did you see?" I asked.

"It was a big circle of light, with a giant black spot in the center."

Ahh . . . I recognized what that ring of light meant.

The poor man's eyes had seen a totally out-of-focus image of the planet. What if Galileo . . . ?

Another group of students, in a small village just over the mountains from Mombasa and the coast, pointed out the Pleiades to me. "The Seven Sisters," they said, using a name invented by the Greeks, and passed on by the Arabs, for the six—not seven—stars visible to the naked eye. "When they set at sunset, it means the rainy season is about to begin." The rainy season meant more than just planting crops to them; the shift in winds had meant, up until less than a hundred years ago, that the slave traders would be returning to Arabia and their grandparents could come out of hiding.

Some schools had electricity, or boasted slide projectors powered by car batteries. In these places I brought slides of the planets, showing the best telescope views and the latest spacecraft images.

"Here's a Voyager Spacecraft image of Io, a moon of Jupiter. Notice this patch of light next to it? An engineer at the Jet Propulsion Laboratory, Linda Moribito, was doing spacecraft navigation when she discovered this and recognized it as a volcanic plume. Just like Kenya, Io has volcanoes. When she reported this . . ."

"She? She?" An electric excitement ran through the crowd of students at a girls' school, run by African nuns in a little town north of Eldoret. I said nothing; my Peace Corps friend Brooke Smith, running the slide projector, just smiled. Maybe some of her students would take science classes a little more seriously now.

Repeating the story the next night at the boys' school down the road, I got a different response. "Oh, sir," said one of the senior boys with grave seriousness. "You should not have allowed that *woman* to make such a discovery."

Kenya was developing, visibly, before my eyes. But for all the influx of roads and telephones, the biggest changes were social changes . . . changes of attitude, of expectations, of self-awareness. My next-door neighbor in the University apartments, himself an African academic and the son of a doctor, was far harsher on Kenyans than I would ever be. "The way we fail to respect women, or treat them as equals, is certainly shameful," he told me one evening in his apartment. His wife, meanwhile, stayed silent in the kitchen, making us tea and chapatis.

What the Africans lacked most was self-confidence. At a lecture at the University of Nairobi on agriculture, a speaker pointed out the similarities between the climate of Kenya and that of California. Yet, he said, land in California had 10 times the yield of that in Kenya. "Why is this?" the speaker asked, rhetorically.

"Because we're Africans," came a voice from the back of the auditorium.

The fear of thinking for one's self was most visible in the University students. Less than one percent of all students get to enter the University; those who make it do so by hard work and memorization. Original thought does not test well.

"Two of my students just came in here," Dr. Maina-Ayiera, my office mate, said to me one day. He was an African who had gotten his Ph.D. in physics at Boston College. "They were telling me that my assigned homework was too difficult. 'Oh sir,' they said, 'we have looked through every book in the library and cannot find the answers!' " He shook his head in disgust.

Without self-confidence, all the trappings of outside aid and development only seemed to mock the Africans, by emphasizing what they couldn't do for themselves. As a result, too many of them gave up hoping they'd ever be able to accomplish anything on their own, and a lot of their talent and energy was lost to despair. It's a truism of "liberation theology" that you can't save a soul when a body is starving. But you can't save a body if the soul is starving, either.

The fact that I was a researcher from MIT meant a lot to these people. The fact that they could share in discovery meant even more.

Esoteric research is important even in a country where people were starving. In its own funny way, my work on the moons of Jupiter was food for the soul. Everyone, from University students to the half-blind old men upcountry, hungered for knowledge. They hungered to be able to feel that they, poor Africans, could also participate in answering the big questions of what and where and how; that they could stand tall at the century's proudest moment; that they, too, were part of the same human race that had touched the Moon.

The hardest part of the Peace Corps was coming home. But with my experience teaching in Nairobi I was able to snag a job teaching physics at Lafayette College, a small liberal-arts school in Pennsylvania. (Meanwhile, the software firm my friends had been working with had gone belly-up, as Lotus and Microsoft took over the spreadsheet market. Not taking that job turned out to be a great business move.)

I loved teaching. I loved the small college atmosphere. I loved the students I worked with, and the students I lived with as the faculty resident of the McKelvy honors house.

And I'd fallen in love, once again, with the stars. The little telescope I had brought with me to Africa got me outdoors at night, looking up and dreaming. Dan Davis taught me how to use that telescope; together we even wrote a book to tell others how to observe the skies. It meant spending a lot of time at Dan's house. All the more I envied his family life, and though I enjoyed my writing and my teaching I felt something missing in my own.

I also stayed in touch with my fellow returned Peace Corps volunteers. One weekend found me in Pittsburgh, visiting my friends Paul and Renee. They'd fallen in love while in Africa, and now they were busy planning their wedding. As the evening went on, we got to reminiscing about our Peace Corps experience. And I recognized what was missing from my life.

It wasn't simply loneliness; I realized, much to my surprise, that I didn't particularly want to have a girlfriend, or be married. Instead, I remembered why being a scientist in the Peace Corps had been special. Simply by being a member of that volunteer group, I had been able to make a statement about the values I thought were important even while I went about my ordinary daily work. I missed that.

Paul and Renee, like my other married friends, were living for each other. Dan and Léonie were also living for their young but growing family. I had met a few rare scientists who lived for pure knowledge. I had yuppie friends who lived for material goods and prestige.

Rather than criticizing them, I had to admit that they at least had something that was the core of their lives. What was the most important thing to me?

Astronomy? Not by itself. My religion was . . . my religion. Still.

As I lay on Paul's floor the next morning, all these thoughts went through my mind. Suddenly the call of the Jesuits was back, stronger than ever.

I went through a routine that by now had become familiar. "Well, God?" I asked. "How about it? Not yet, huh?"

"Now."

Oh? I went through my litany . . . was I motivated by the same weak reasons? I wasn't trying to run away from an unhappy situation. In fact, I loved my position at Lafayette. I wasn't hungry for respect; as a physics professor I already had a degree of respect, even from other professors, that I found almost silly. And further, after being out in the world for 20 years I no longer had an adolescent awe of the clergy.

Religion aside, was I suited to do this job that I was thinking of getting into? After all, what would I have to do, day to day? To teach? But I was a teacher already, and I loved it. To deal with people with problems? But I did exactly that as an advisor to the honors students; I had learned to deal firsthand with problems far more serious than I had ever run away from at Boston College. To live and work with the poor? In the Peace Corps I'd been trained to work with the poor, and I'd lived with third-world poverty close up for 2 years.

Should I become a Franciscan? Or join the Irish brothers I'd met who taught in Africa? That was attractive; I really wanted to be a brother, not a priest.

But I remembered Jesuit brothers back in high school, and the Jesuit scientists I'd known, and the constant calling specifically to that order that I'd felt for 20 years. The answer seemed obvious.

As the months passed, the calling got stronger.

I brought it up with Dan and Léonie. Dan refused to give me any advice. "When I was a kid, I always wanted to be a Jesuit astronomer myself," he told me. "So I could hardly give you an unbiased opinion. Why don't you talk it over with Léonie?" he asked. "She knows you as well as I do."

So Léonie and I made a date to go out to dinner, by ourselves, and talk it over at length. She came right to the point.

"Why do you want to be a Jesuit?" she asked.

I admitted, rather sheepishly, "I'm not sure. I'm suspicious myself of my motives. It's like anything else. Like joining the Peace Corps; I have both good and bad reasons."

"What are the bad ones?"

"Well," I admitted, "part of it is simply that I enjoy the trappings of my religion. The rituals and prayers, you know. I just like the idea of living in a community where those ceremonies would be available. Where I can get to Mass every day."

Léo looked at me, puzzled. "Explain to me again why that's a bad reason?"

"It's too easy. I'd enjoy it too much. I . . . hmm. Uh, maybe you have a point."

By that summer, the call was overwhelming. Every month that passed, I became more confident and content in my decision. My life had given me wealth, love, and freedom. Nothing could make me happier than to pass them on.

God has a strange sense of humor—that's one of the things I like so much about Him. But the God I knew so well did not litter false clues about one's life to fool or trap people. Looking back over my crazy-looking path, it didn't seem so crazy after all. Instead, I saw a pattern, directing me to live the life I'd led, to learn from the experiences that have been sent my way, to become the person I had become.

I was an astronomer, a teacher, a physicist, a researcher. A man born in America of Italian and Irish ancestry. A Catholic. And on August 16, 1989, I crossed the threshold of the Jesuit novitiate in Wernersville, Pennsylvania, and I became a Jesuit.

JUSTICE IN THE OCEANS OF EUROPA

OW HAS being a Jesuit affected my life as a scientist? Well . . . about 15 years ago, I was thumbing through a misfiled book in the science section of a local bookstore. A science popularizer, a writer of sufficient intelligence and talent that one wonders why he was afraid to try his hand at legitimate reporting, had produced an entire book about the so-called face on Mars (a particular outcrop on the ruddy planet that, under odd lighting, seems to reveal a strangely humanoid visage) and, most especially, the NASA conspiracy to suppress the evidence of cities on Mars. (A "successful NASA conspiracy" requires even more credulity than a face on Mars.)

What caught my eye, however, was the blurb about the author on the back cover. "He was also the first person to propose that life could exist in oceans under the ice crust of Europa!"

I could only shake my head. "Not only are his ideas crackpot," I said to myself, "but he stole them from me!"

Which is only partially untrue. Yes, in my thesis on the icy moons of Jupiter, published in 1975—5 years before his article on the topic—I did propose that Europa had a liquid ocean under its surface, and I even speculated on the possibility of life in such an ocean. But I doubt he stole the idea from me. I doubt he ever even heard of me, or my thesis . . . or any of the other literature on the subject, either.

The history of this particular crackpot idea, my contribution to crank science, started in 1973 when I was a junior at MIT looking for an undergraduate research project. I chose to work with Professor John Lewis, mostly because I enjoyed his sense of humor. Between the lunchtime conversations at Walker Memorial, and the afternoon Frisbee sessions, working with him was fun.

Lewis had published a paper in 1971 pointing out that the moons of Jupiter and Saturn were probably made of rock and water ice and, if so, the radioactive elements decaying in the rock could provide enough heat to melt the ice. That could lead to an interesting internal structure.

His idea was simply a rough sketch, a back-of-the-envelope calculation of the type used by scientists all the time to try out a new idea. Back in the early 1970s, what did we know about the moons of Jupiter and Saturn? Not much.

There was some reason to believe the surfaces were covered with water ice. They appeared to be bright, like the clouds of Jupiter; and indeed by the mid-1970s the first infrared spectra had been taken, showing the distinctive colors of water ice present on the three outer bodies. The brightest and iciest was Europa, then Ganymede, then Callisto. (At that point, Io was still an enigma.)

But were they rocky bodies with just a thin ice coating, or were they icy through and through? There were some crude estimates of their mass (based on how the moons perturbed each others' orbits) and some equally crude estimates of their sizes. The mass divided by the volume gave the density; that could be compared against the densities of ice and rock.

When we did the calculation for Jupiter's four major moons, the ones discovered by Galileo, we found that the outermost one, Callisto, was about 60 percent ice; Ganymede, next in, was made up of roughly equal parts ice and rock, while Europa was probably 90 percent rock and only 10 percent ice. Io, the innermost moon, had a bright surface like Europa but no evidence of water ice; something else must be causing its high reflectivity. One curious result was that the moon with the brightest, iciest surface, Europa, turned out to be mostly rock; while the moon with the darkest, presumably rockiest surface, Callisto, had the most ice in its makeup.

These proportions fit nicely into John Lewis's ideas for the formation of planets and moons. He envisioned a "solar nebula," a cloud of gas and dust around the Sun, hot at the center and cooler toward the edges. Inner planets would be mostly rocky, while outer planets would be formed of material that was cold enough to include ices and thereby make themselves massive enough to trap the nebular gas, thus becoming gas giants. In the same way, a cloud of gas and dust trapped by the growing Jupiter should also be hotter as one got closer to Jupiter; thus the proportion of ice in each moon should increase as one went out, away from Jupiter, into the colder regions of this proto-jovian nebula.

To determine whether any of these icy moons might actually melt, Lewis worked out a simple model. He assumed that: (1) all the heat generated inside the moons would come from the decay of radioactive elements in the rocky material and (2) those radioactive elements would be found there in the same proportions and abundances as they are found in ordinary meteorites today. He also assumed that: (3) the rocky material and the ice were uniformly mixed throughout the moon and (4) whatever heat was generated inside the moons was exactly balanced by the heat radiating off the surface of the moon— the interior was neither heating up nor cooling off, but in steady state. And he assumed that: (5) heat flowed out of the moon, up to the surface, by conduction.

Every one of those assumptions seemed pretty reasonable, but none was certain. The trouble is, these were a lot of assumptions. Even if each one had a 90 percent chance of being correct, there was less than a 60 percent chance that all five would be correct simultaneously.

To find the final temperature inside the moon, Lewis set up an equation for the rate at which heat was generated inside the moon, and set it equal (assumption 4) to the rate that it flowed out of the moon. The heat generated equaled the heat per gram, Q, generated by radioactive materials in a meteorite (assumptions 1 and 2), times the fraction of the moon that was rocky, f (assumption 3), times the mass of the moon—which is the density times the volume of the moon [$(4/3)\rho\pi r^3$, where r is the radius of the moon]. The heat that flows out is determined by the temperature gradient in the moon, the amount the temperature increases for every meter inside ($\Delta T/\Delta r$ or, in the language of calculus, dT/dr), times the conductivity K of the ice/rock mixture (assumption 5), times the surface area that the heat can flow through ($4\pi r^2$, the surface area of a sphere).

Thus, the heat in, $(4/3)fQ\rho\pi r^3$, is set equal to the heat out, or $(dT/dr)4\pi Kr^2$; do the algebra to get $dT/dr = fQ\rho\pi r/3K$. From that you can insert the values of the density and radius and so forth, integrate the equation, and calculate the temperature rise above the ambient temperature at any point inside a body.

Now, there are all sorts of shortcomings to this calculation. It should not be taken as true, but merely one way to answer the question, "is there any hope that the interior might be molten?" And the answer was an unequivocal, "maybe."

To do the calculation correctly, we really needed to model the whole evolution of the moon. After all, once the moon's interior did start to melt, the rocky material would fall through the water to form a core at the center of the moon . . . carrying the heat sources away (and adding heat from the release of gravitational energy during the core formation). Once molten, water transports heat by convection, not conduction. The amount of heat generated by radioactive decay will itself decay, as the amount of radioactive isotopes decays; thus the steady-state assumption could be seriously wrong. Furthermore, we needed to account for the heat of fusion needed to turn ice into water (and back, should the moon start to freeze up again). And, finally, it turns out that the moons of Jupiter are so large that the ice in their interiors is not the same as the ice we're familiar with under ordinary conditions, but various phases of high-pressure ice. The values of the densities, conductivities, and heat capacities of these phases are different from those of ordinary ice; and they all vary as the temperature of the ice varies.

The only way to solve such a messy problem was by computer. Professor Lewis asked me: would I be interested in writing a computer model to take all these effects into account? It kept me busy for the next 3 years.

In the end, I came up with a model that predicted a bit of melting inside Callisto, but otherwise described for it a several-hundred-kilometer thick crust that probably never evolved, consistent with the dark rock/ice mixture inferred for its surface; more melting and a thinner crust on Ganymede, since it appeared to have more rock and so more heat in its interior. Europa was, by my model, totally melted, with maybe 100 kilometers of water and a thin icy crust over a rocky core almost as big as Earth's Moon.

In an appendix in this thesis, I noted that this rock would have been in intimate contact with the mantle of water (and whatever would be dissolved in that water). It would probably be big enough to have all sorts of geological evolution, like lava flows, occurring inside. In general, it would be a geochemist's delight of possible reactions, easily comparable to the complexity of Earth's salty oceans. Indeed, if "rocky" material were as rich in carbon as some of the primitive meteorites were, Europa could even have the beginnings of organic chemistry.

The last sentence of my thesis, written in an arch tone of pompous adolescent cleverness, read: ". . . we stop short of postulating life forms in these mantles; we leave such to others more experienced than ourselves in such speculations." So actually, I guess I was the first person to deliberately *not* propose life in the oceans of Europa.

I knew whom I meant by those more experienced "others." Carl Sagan had been pushing the possibility of life in every conceivable place (and some inconceivable ones) for years. Just the mere presence of water on its surface had been enough for him to speculate in passing about life on Europa, as early as 1971. Imagine my shock when I discovered that the opening night of the Jupiter conference in 1975, where I would be presenting this work for the first time in public, was being chaired by Carl Sagan.

I had a chance to chat with him briefly before the session, and I ended our conversation with the suggestion that this ocean was a place to look for life. He gave me a condescending smile. "Life needs energy, sunlight," he reminded me. "How are you going to get sunlight through a thick crust of ice?"

I was crushed. Well, not too crushed . . . I really didn't believe there'd be life there, anyway. But still, it was such an obvious point, I should have thought of it myself. No sunlight, of course there'd be no life. But maybe, I thought to myself, wouldn't those core volcanoes provide enough energy? Nahh . . . who'd ever heard of life living off the energy of a volcano?

I presented my paper, to polite applause (it was the last talk of a long night) and mentioned in passing, during the Q&A session, how I had thought there might be life deep in those oceans. "But Dr. Sagan pointed out, there's no energy source for them—no sunlight down there." It got about all the attention I expected.

That was 1975. Four years later, in 1979, the Voyager spacecraft passed Jupiter and sent back the first detailed images of my moons. And they saw everything I had predicted! A dark primitive Callisto, a partially resurfaced Ganymede, and Europa completely covered with a fresh-looking surface of ice.

Unfortunately, it also sent back more accurate values for the masses and sizes. I had said Callisto would look different from Ganymede because it had less rock. The new numbers showed that it had just as much rock as Ganymede. Oops.

Voyager also found active volcanoes on Io. Theorists had recently predicted that tidal stresses, the flexing of Io by Jupiter's gravity, would produce orders of magnitude more heat inside it than you'd get from mere radioactive decay. Further work suggested that Europa should also be heated, to some extent, by this process.

Other theorists looking at ice suggested that, not only does liquid water convect instead of conduct heat, but that warm ice should also convect.

In other words, my models succeeded in predicting what we saw, but for all the wrong reasons. Virtually all of our starting assumptions had turned out to be wrong. My model for Callisto was just plain wrong, based on bad numbers. My model for Europa underestimated the amount of heat in (neglecting tides) and also underestimated the rate the heat would escape (neglecting convection). That the two errors canceled each other was just dumb luck. My model itself was worthless.

Meanwhile, in the late 1970s, a group of oceanographers studying volcanic vents under the Atlantic discovered whole colonies of life forms that take their energy from the chemical reaction between the erupting lava and the seawater it's erupting into. Life does indeed exist where the Sun never reaches.

In 1983, a bunch of scientists in California (including a former student of Carl Sagan) published a paper that put it all together . . . the idea of Europan oceans suggested by the Voyager images, the heat source of tides, the possibility of life living off lava flows. They predicted that the oceans of Europa would be a good place to look for life.

They didn't reference my thesis (though they did reference the crackpot whom I mentioned at the beginning of this chapter). I got no credit for thinking of the possibility of life. Was I ticked off? Of course. Did I have any right to be ticked off? Absolutely not.

My prediction of life was based on a fatally flawed theory, backed up by no serious calculations, that ignored a major piece of the puzzle. By contrast, the California scientists (Ray Reynolds, Steve Squyres, D. S. Colburn, and Chris McKay) attacked the whole problem, and did it right. They, and they alone, deserve the credit. They did science. By contrast, all I had done was science fiction.

So, that being the case, why was I so ticked off at them? Because I felt they had poached on my moons. Yes, mine. All mine! After years of working on a thesis about those places I had a deep-seated, and wholly irrational, feeling that I owned those places. Shades of Galileo and Grassi . . .

That sort of madness was not mine alone. I ran into it in other scientists working on the moons of Jupiter. This sort of jovian lunacy seemed contagious. We all jealously guarded what we had done, and bitterly attacked each other for daring to stray on that turf. And since they were bigger and tougher and meaner than me, their attacks were more effective than mine. That's when I finally quit it all and left to join the Peace Corps.

It was insane. I remember once, walking down the streets of Nairobi having long left that competitive world behind, still plotting in my head the destruction of those evil men who had dared steal my moons from me. Suddenly, as from a dream, I looked up and saw the blue skies and the exotic scenery. Thanks to them, I'd joined the Peace Corps, and being in the Peace Corps was the most fun I'd had in years. Thanks to them! I did a quick turn into a coffeeshop, had a cup of fresh-brewed Kenya double-A, and decided that being happy really was the sweetest revenge.

Over that cup of coffee, I thought even further about scientific fights I'd known, not only my own but others' as well. And it became clear that fighting for priority, fighting for recognition, was a fool's game. No one ever won. Worse, it meant that the prize was not learning about the Universe, it was merely "fame and glory." And if all I wanted from life was fame and glory, boy was I in the wrong business!

But years later, as a Jesuit studying the philosophy of justice and the theology of ethics, I came to an even bolder realization. Not only was it pointless to try to fight for my "rights" of priority and recognition; it was, ultimately, unjustifiable.

I recalled a paper I had come across several years earlier ("The Nature and Value of Rights" in *The Journal of Value Inquiry*) by the philosopher Joel Feinberg. In it, he rhetorically asked his reader to conduct a bizarre thought experiment:

> Try to imagine Nowheresville—a world very much like our own except that no one . . . has rights. If this makes Nowheresville too ugly to hold very long in contemplation, we can make it as pretty as we wish in other moral respects . . . fill this imagined world with as much benevolence, compassion, sympathy, and pity as it will conveniently hold without strain . . . We can imagine men helping one another from compassionate motives merely, quite as much or even more than they do in our actual world from a variety of more complicated motives . . .
>
> Nowheresvillians, even when they are discriminated against invidiously, or left without the things they need, or otherwise badly treated, do not think to leap to their feet and make righteous demands against one another . . .

"Try to imagine a world where no one has rights," asked Feinberg. But it was clear that he couldn't imagine such a world himself. It was, he believed, nowhere. And yet, without addressing just what is meant by rights or for whom rights exist, Feinberg missed seeing a world where, indeed, no rights exist.

Because, as a matter of fact, I claim that I can claim nothing by right.

Note how I am phrasing this. I claim . . . I do not state that everyone must claim this. I would certainly not object if other individuals adopt my sense of personal justice; but I do not insist, demand, try to enforce, or even expect anyone else to do so. In defining a personal system of ethics, I can state only those principles that I personally intuit contain the ways in which I personally must live.

"I claim no rights." The general principle can be expanded: I neither demand nor expect any return for favors, or any recognition, for the things I accomplish or the good I do for others. Likewise, I accept favors with no expectations on myself. With no rights comes no duties. That may sound like selfishness, but in fact it's just the opposite. In some ways, it's the hardest part of living this style of life.

I know, because I'm not talking about some theoretical "how-I-wish-I-lived" ideal. This is my actual day-to-day experience now as a Jesuit, and the experience of every member of a religious order who lives entirely on the donations of others.

It's similar to (but even deeper than) the experience of a family member who's living, at least at the moment, on the income of someone else in their house. A child living off parents (or vice versa) is united by ties of love and ties of blood. But I know that thousands of people, virtually all of them total strangers to me and many living under financial conditions far more severe than mine, have donated the money that buys my burgers and pays my electric bill. And when friends take me out to dinner, both they and I know that there's no way I can ever pay them back. I have no income. (Indeed, even the proceeds from this book are going to a nonprofit foundation, not to me.)

Granted, others might expect a return for the favors they do me. However, under this system I cannot feel an obligation to meet their expectations. This leads to a host of practical questions—do I pay for

the food I eat in a restaurant? That must be addressed. Before I
address them, however, let's try to figure out where this odd idea "I
have no rights" comes from.

I did nothing to earn life; I did nothing to earn my abilities.
Indeed, even if I hunt my own food, I did not create the animals that
I hunt; if I grow my own produce, planting and watering and harvest-
ing in season, still I did not create the plants whose internal chemistry
is such that they are actually able to sustain my life. I certainly did not
create the planet or its climate that can support such life. The warmth
and the air and the water that I take for granted are, in fact, rare in this
solar system. All of this has been a gift to me. I know, intuitively, that
I have no right to any of it.

Where does this sense or intuition come from? In other words,
what is the "teleology" behind my axiom, "I claim no rights"? In my
case it is my personal theology, my choice to buy in completely to
the Christian world view (or, at least, my own peculiar understanding of it).

I accept the Church because, to quote T. S. Eliot, she tells me
important things that I am not likely to learn on my own:

> She tells them of Life and Death, and of all that they would forget.
> She is tender where they would be hard, and hard where they would
> be soft. She tells them of Evil and Sin, and other unpleasant facts.

(This quote is from one of the choruses in his play, *The Rock*.) One
of these unpleasant facts I accept is that everything I have and everything I am is an unjustified gift. I reject the pelagian idea that I can, by
my own actions, become deserving of God's love, or any form of
worldly happiness. Rather, the abundant love I receive from God and
all the happiness I experience on Earth, which is God's way of
expressing that love, comes unearned.

Only if I accept the sort of radical poverty that says I have nothing
myself, not even rights, can I see that I have no currency with which
to "trade" for God's gifts, except to respond to his love post facto; and
the proper response to love, is love. The ideal thus develops that all

my actions ought to occur out of love, not duty or obligation. The positive side of "I claim no rights" is that "I act only out of love."

I have chosen a personally radical form of Christianity. It's also a totally unworkable system if I were to prescribe it for everyone. It's not the way that society "ought" to be set up. A society that does protect rights is a good society; it is my duty to support such a society, and to treat others as though they did have rights; and I am thankful when society, and others, treat me in that way. I am thankful precisely because it is a gift . . . an unexpected, and undeserved, one.

So that's how being a Jesuit has changed the way I do science. I can't do science just looking for credit. I can't even think that it will earn me tenure, or more grants (though either would be nice to receive). The work I do, today, must be its own reward, today. I must do it for the only reason worth doing anything. I must do it for love.

Oh, and so is there life in the oceans of Europa? Beats me. I don't even know if such oceans actually exist or not. I hope some day to get the gift of finding out. But I hope I never think that I deserve to know, much less get "credit" for it. If life forms exist, they'll be God's creatures, not mine.

WOULD YOU BAPTIZE
AN EXTRATERRESTRIAL?

PEAKING OF alien life forms . . . it's one of those questions that we get asked over and over again, mostly by reporters or people who don't know us very well. The *Weekly World News* once ran a story headlined "Missionaries for Mars! Vatican Training Astro-Priests to Spread Gospel to Space Aliens!" And deep down, I suspect some people think that's what the Vatican Observatory is really all about.

It isn't.

But still, we get the questions. It's part of a natural connection, one might even say confusion, between the science of looking at distant stars and the philosophy of worrying about the unknown in its many guises. People think we're looking for philosophical answers with our telescopes. What we're actually doing is inspiring philosophical questions.

It has been posited that the discovery of life elsewhere in the universe would fundamentally change the way we humans think about ourselves. Maybe; but, to borrow an insight from the historian of science Stephen Dick, I suspect that change has already happened. I really don't think anyone who's aware of the science would be fundamentally changed by the discovery, because nearly everyone expects that it will happen eventually. Probably not in our lifetime; maybe not in the next millennium. But eventually.

Finding any sort of life off planet Earth, either bacteria or extraterrestrials, would pose no problem for religion. Stephen Dick has recently written an excellent popular book on the history of how people through the ages have viewed the possibility of extraterrestrials (*Life on Other Worlds*, Cambridge University Press, 1998). He notes that most atheists seem to think discovering extraterrestrial life would be the death of religion; but, in fact, most religious people don't see it that way at all. Indeed, as it happens some of the most prominent scientists currently working on the question of life on Mars are also active churchgoers.

God created the whole universe. There's nothing that makes one place more special than another. Religious people have been able to think in these "cosmic" terms all along, and happily speculated about "other worlds" long before the science fiction crowd had adopted the concept.

But there is one crucial question that will face Christianity if, or when, extraterrestrial intelligence is discovered. That's the question about what the Incarnation means to other species. In other words, would aliens need to have their own version of Jesus?

Do aliens need to be saved? Depends if they are subject to "original sin" or not. The traditional theology of original sin, tracing it back to the origins of the human race, says absolutely nothing about other entities, either way. Once we find other intelligences, we'll be in a better position to expand that theology.

Assuming that original sin, the problem of evil, does face other intelligences, what role does Christian salvation play in their world?

St. Paul's hymns in Colossians 1 and Ephesians 1 make it clear that the resurrection of Christ applies to all creation (". . . everything in the heavens and everything on earth"). It is the definitive salvation event for the cosmos. Another bit of Biblical evidence is the opening of John's Gospel, who tells us that The Word (which is to say, the Incarnation of God) was present from the Beginning; it is part and parcel of the woof and weave of the Universe.

Just how this "Word" might be "spoken" to the rest of the intelligent universe, I don't know. But it will be in "words" (that is, events) appropriate to those beings. In any event, good extraterrestrials (ETs), just like good humans, do not need to know about Christ for salvation; that's the tradition of "baptism by desire."

The point here is that, even though the life of Jesus occurred at a specific space-time point, on a particular world line (to put it in general relativity terms), it also was an event that John's Gospel describes as occurring in the beginning—the one point that is simultaneous in all world lines, and so present in all time and in all space. Thus, there can only be one Incarnation—though various ET civilizations may or may not have experienced that Incarnation in the same way that Earth did.

In science we assume that the laws of physics (which we know so imperfectly yet!) are as true everywhere in the universe as they are in our puny little laboratories here on Earth. Likewise, the "laws" of philosophy or theology—that is to say, the essential truths themselves, not to be confused with the formulas our human languages use to try to express these truths—are the same, and true, everywhere.

One of the big advances that St. Aquinas made was to insist, countering other popular philosophers of the thirteenth century, that there was only one Truth—not one truth for religion, another for science. Truth is one, even though our ways of groping for that truth are manifold. So the formulas we use—mathematical, philosophical, or whatever—can be very different, but they all are trying to get to the same place ultimately.

We have no data about other nonhuman civilizations. They may not even exist; or they may be plentiful. (To insist that "God could not have made other worlds" was declared a heresy back in the thirteenth century—so this even covers alternate or parallel universes!) ETs may not be aware of the idea of an Incarnation, or they may have their own experience of the matter. Their experience may be so alien from ours that even though they have experienced God in their own way, it's an experience that we will never be able to share, nor they share in our experience.

I would suspect, though, that any conscious entity would wonder about the same things we wonder about—origins, meaning, etc.—and, just as we can learn from other cultures here on Earth, I would hope we could learn from other ET cultures.

Inevitably, any interaction with an unfamiliar culture results in some sort of evangelization. I recall my days in the Peace Corps, where kids in rural Africa would start adopting American customs, like wearing blue jeans, just because the Peace Corps teacher at their school wore blue jeans—even when the teacher tried not to influence the students!

So the question of whether or not one should evangelize is really a moot point. Any aliens we find will learn and change from contact with us, just as we will learn and change from contact with them. It's inevitable. And they'll be evangelizing us, too.

If we came across an ET culture that insisted $2 + 2 = 5$, then we'd have to assume that either what they meant by 5 is what we meant by 4, or that one of us was seriously in error! Obviously we'd want to explore the matter further. "Evangelization" is what I would call this "exploration." We would clearly want to tell ETs what we have learned; we also want to listen to them, to hear what they have learned.

But one thing I know personally I have learned from studying eastern religions is that they have shown me the unique things that Christianity has, which I always took for granted and never realized other cultures might not have had . . . for instance, the sense of a universe that is good, a creation of God, worth studying and worth caring for, and that one can come closer to God by immersing one's self in this universe (rather than trying to reject the physical world).

To withhold from an ET civilization a part of us as fundamental to ourselves as our religions—plural—would be dishonest, and certainly it would show no respect for them as equals. The important message that every Christian missionary has carried to each culture is that all people are equal and all of them are heirs to the knowledge of God that has been given to us. Soldiers might conquer them, secular philosophers might treat them as less than human (or, worse, condescend to them as "noble savages") but the missionary can only accept them as equals.

Frankly, if you think about it, any creatures on any other planets, subject to the same laws of chemistry and physics as us, made of the same kinds of atoms, with an awareness and a will recognizably like ours, would be at the very least our cousins in the cosmos. They would be so similar to us in all the essentials that I don't think you'd even have the right to call them aliens.

PART FOUR

WIDE WILD WHITENESS

WELL MET AT ANSMET

EVERAL YEARS ago, I got a brief fax from a meteorite scientist in Japan named Keizo Yanai, asking for a small piece (less than a gram) of Chassigny. Chassigny is a Martian meteorite, and of those from Mars it's probably one of the rarest, for a lot of chemical reasons I need not go into here. My initial reaction had been, "No way!" Even then, it was worth something like $1000 a gram (and after the life-on-Mars sample, ALH84001, hit the news the value tripled).

But the name "Yanai" rang a bell. I looked it up, and sure enough, he had been the author of several of the Japanese Antarctic Meteorite catalogs. Furthermore, in our collection at the Vatican we had two subgram pieces of Chassigny, too small to display (we do also have a larger hand specimen) but plenty big enough for research purposes. We really wouldn't miss one of them. And I figured at the time it would be a nice gesture. Maybe he'd let me come measure the densities of his meteorites some day. So I sent him a piece.

Later I learned that Yanai had been the chief scientist with the Japanese Antarctic meteorite program. He was the one who, 25 years ago, realized that the blue ice fields of Antarctica were embedded with thousands of meteorites. For nearly 20 years he collected the Japanese Antarctic meteorites, expanding the world's collection of meteorites several times over. In the fall of 1996 I had a special reason to be thinking about him . . .

On a gray November evening, I met René Martinez and Sara Russell in a dingy bar at the Los Angeles airport.

It was no chance meeting. We'd arranged it by e-mail, and I'd probably walked through that bar three times, trying to make eye contact with half a dozen people, before René and I finally decided that, maybe, we were the guys looking for each other. Sara joined us soon after; she knew René, so that made it easier for her to find us.

When our flight was called, we took our separate seats, scattered among 400 others on the 747. Together again at the Auckland, New Zealand, airport, we figured out how to get through customs and past the friendly drug-sniffing puppy dogs to catch our flight to the South Island. (The airline lost René's luggage; no surprise.) The fact that Sara had done this all once before was supposed to help; it didn't.

In Christchurch, New Zealand, we caught a shuttle to the pre-arranged motel.

A few hours later, we met up with Ralph Harvey, the principal investigator (PI) and fearless leader of our little group. (He was at a neighboring motel with Nancy, newly wed, just finishing their honeymoon.)

Laurie Leshin joined us at the motel that evening; she had done a tour of New Zealand the week before we arrived.

Our sixth, John Schutt, was already waiting for us, 2000 miles further south, at McMurdo Base.

Antarctica.

We six were the 1996 ANSMET team: the Antarctic Search for Meteorites expedition. This was the twentieth year the U.S. National

Science Foundation had sponsored scientists like us to go to the ice to pick up rocks that had fallen from space.

Christchurch, the main town on the southern island of New Zealand, is the jumping-off point for most people flying to Antarctica. It's the closest airport to McMurdo, the largest "city" on the icy continent. The International Antarctic Center—the IAC—is located adjacent to the airport in Christchurch. It represents teams from the United States, New Zealand, Italy, and the United Nations. There we would pick up our cold-weather clothing and our last supplies from civilization before heading south.

We had arrived on a Friday afternoon (losing a day to the dateline). Early Saturday morning we ventured to the IAC to get ourselves fitted out for the ice. They had received a list of our approximate sizes months ago, but they asked (again) where we were going and gave us a pile of the sorts of clothes they thought we'd need. There were about 20 of us there that morning, three or four different teams of scientists heading to the continent, including a crew I'd seen in the airport in Los Angeles. At least two sets of us were going to be living on the ice itself . . . the harshest duty. But we were the only team that would be spending 6 weeks in tents, on the windiest part of the plateau. We got the biggest pile of clothes.

"Rule One: Remember, you have to carry all this stuff," our fearless leader Ralph warned me.

I started thinking of which things I could do without.

"Remember, whatever you don't take now, you can't get down there. That's also Rule One."

Two pairs of long johns. Overkill? Or not enough for 6 weeks without doing laundry? About 12 pairs of gloves, in every imaginable size, shape, thickness, design, and material. Which ones would I prefer once I got there? I wouldn't know 'til I'd tried them all.

On Monday morning we got up early and caught a shuttle to the IAC, at the airport. There we dressed in all our warmest gear (as instructed), packed what was left into two orange bags (one carry on, one "checked"), and stored what we wouldn't be bringing along at the IAC for our eventual return. Then we stood around while our luggage was inspected by more drug-sniffing dogs (Antarctica is no place to get high) and waited.

After more than an hour, we finally piled into buses that took us out to the runway. More waiting while our baggage was strapped into the back of a Kiwi Air Force C-130 cargo plane. Then we filed in, strapping ourselves like so much cargo in the front of the same plane. They passed out sack lunches and earplugs. The engines roared; and we took off.

Only a few tiny portholes gave light to the interior, and we sat along the wall with our backs to them. Forty of us were heading down to the ice, along with a flight crew of a dozen Kiwis. Two engineers climbed over our baggage to look out the tiny windows at the engines on the wings, making certain they were still there (something I don't recall them ever doing on TWA). And then the plane made a graceful banking turn, settled down, and came in for a smooth landing.

Back at Christchurch.

Filing out, I looked for myself. All the engines still seemed to be attached, as far as I could see. Nonetheless, we stood on the tarmac till nearly noon, dressed for Antarctica in the ever-growing heat of a Christchurch November day. Ralph, the old hand, had warned us . . . we could be leaving at any moment, or the flight could be postponed several days.

"You won't see your checked luggage until we get to McMurdo, even if it's days from now," he had said.

But we did get off, just a little after noon. The flight was 8 hours, at 300 miles an hour, in an unpressurized, unsoundproofed military plane, sitting on benches designed to have parachutes between you and the seat, crammed together like sardines, where conversation or listening to music was impossible (the engines were so loud). And the sack lunches included packets of chocolate pudding, but no spoons. Last time I fly that airline!

It was just after 8 p.m., almost dark, by the time we reached McMurdo. Indeed, sundown was a mere . . . 3 months away. Well, it felt dark. It felt like night. McMurdo's sunshine did look different in the evening.

We landed on the Ross ice shelf, in sight of McMurdo itself. A couple of large buses with huge tires designed to drive on the ice and snow were waiting to take us to the cafeteria, where dinner had been held over for us. From there, we picked up the keys to our dorm rooms and went to settle in for the night.

Exhaustion fought excitement. From moment to moment, one or the other held the upper hand. I was pooped. This was Antarctica! I wanted to unpack and surround myself with familiar things; crawl into bed with a tape player. And I wanted to get out and see everything, at once!

McMurdo felt strange. The air seemed thin, like we were at 10,000 feet, but the ice shelf next to us was obvious proof we were actually at sea level. Strange smells, too; no vegetation to cover the odor of diesel fuels outdoors, and the musk of mildew from damp blankets and carpets pervaded all the dormitory rooms.

The temperature felt not much different from a small town in Michigan in midwinter, hovering in the low 20s. The roads were black gravel (from local volcanic rock), the road traffic mostly big orange work trucks with Idaho license plates and an occasional monster-wheeled vehicle ("Ivan the terra-bus"); they reminded me of the Tonka Toys I played with as a kid.

An odd mixture of quonset huts and military-base wooden structures lined the streets, along with a set of ugly multistory dorms painted olive green, big enough to house nearly a thousand soldiers (or, nowadays, civilians) in close quarters. Next to them stood the ultramodern white aluminum Creary Science Center—a spacious and beautifully equipped laboratory building. Creary was the local home for scientists like us—"beakers," the regulars called us. A street sign, swiped from Greenwich Village and slightly modified, labeled the dirt path in front of Creary, "Beeker Street."

We stayed a week on base. I was exhausted every moment of it. What strength the physical work didn't do in, the mental anxiety sapped.

We had lots of little tasks to do. Meetings to go to: how to survive on the ice, how to check out cross country skis (never got around to that), how to make phone calls home, how to get into our office at the Creary Labs. Things to plan: Ralph laid out maps and photos to show us where we'd be exploring. Techniques to learn: John Schutt gave us basic training on ropes and knots and systems of pulleys. Thank God, finally something I already knew; thanks to living around boats all my life, I wasn't tied up in knots by knots.

We put boxes together, then filled them with food to last 6-weeks-plus (just in case the trip home got delayed by bad weather). I made sure we took plenty of chocolate. Then we painted labels on the boxes so they'd arrive with us on the ice. We were equipped with extra gear, crampons for our boots and a pack full of ropes, an ice pick, and a pair of binoculars. We went to snowmobile school—learned how the engines worked and how to fix them when they didn't, how to start them in the morning and keep them warm and fueled, and finally how to drive them without killing yourself. We checked out our tents and kitchen gear. And we prepared a dozen Nansen sleds with pallets and ropes to carry all our stuff.

And in back of it all, hovering over everything we did, was that damned Mars rock.

This was November of 1996. Three months earlier, an eager group of NASA scientists had confirmed a report, prematurely leaked to the press, that they'd found evidence consistent with fossil life in the meteorite Allan Hills 84001. It was the sensation of the year. And we were caught up in the middle of it, in all too many ways.

This meteorite had been found by an ANSMET expedition 12 years earlier. In fact, the woman who'd picked it up, Robbie Score, was living and working at McMurdo now as the local administrator of the science programs (including ours). She was an old buddy of nearly everyone, especially René with whom she'd worked at the Johnson Space Center in Houston.

The possible life fossils in ALH84001 were being ballyhooed as a justification of our whole meteorite expedition. In the public eye, the six of us were down here to "look for more Mars rocks with life in them."

We almost all of us had a history of some sort with that rock.

My one big meteorite paper back in the 1970s had set the stage for using geochemistry to identify certain meteorites as Martian rocks. Now, as the Vatican's only meteorite expert, I was being quoted in the press about the "theological and philosophical significance" (none that I could see!) of a discovery I wasn't even sure I believed.

John Schutt was part of the team that found it in 1984.

René's coworkers were the ones claiming they'd seen the fossils.

Laurie Leshin's work on hydrogen and oxygen isotopes in that rock were being used by both the pro- and antilife camps to justify their claims.

And Ralph Harvey had, just that summer, 1 month before the NASA group's announcement, published a paper attempting to prove that the rock was formed at high temperature. If he was right, life in that rock would have been impossible. His ANSMET program, as it turned out, would be the biggest beneficiary of the ALH84001 hoopla, while at the same time he was perhaps the most outspoken skeptic of the whole result. So much for the cynics who thought the announcement was just a stunt by NASA to get more funding.

(Only Sara Russell was innocent of any connection. An expert on extinct radionuclides in meteorites, some of them older than the solar system itself, she merely sniffed at all the excitement over this mere 4-billion-year-old rock. Whatever opinion she had about the life evidence, she kept to herself.)

There's not much to do in McMurdo. Outside of a bar and a coffeehouse, a library that's open only during odd hours, and a cafeteria that's likewise only open a few hours a day, there aren't many places to go except to work or back to the room you share with one to five other people . . . who soon become just as sick of you as you are of them. So when Ralph was asked to talk about ALH84001, he packed the cafeteria with a full audience. He gave a good talk; he explained the science, and the controversy, in clear and (for him) relatively civil terms. Of course, afterwards, this just added to our notoriety on base.

Next morning, at breakfast, Laurie and Sara overheard a conversation at the table next to ours. "I found out why that guy last night was so down on life from Mars," one of the local technicians said. "Turns out, he's from the Vatican!" The other nodded, knowingly.

Poor Ralph.

Of course, that also made it clear to me just how careful I had to be when discussing my views on the whole Mars life issue. No matter what I said, people would read an agenda into it.

It also pointed out the generally naïve view of religion that most people had at McMurdo. Not surprising, considering that the average age of the inhabitants was probably around 25. At 44, I was one of the older people on the base. There weren't many married couples, and no children were allowed (16 was the minimum age to come to Antarctica, I think I was told). And it wasn't a climate that many older folks could tolerate for long. That added to the strange atmosphere of the base, and went a long way to explain the reactions I got to being a Jesuit scientist among them.

There was a chapel at McMurdo and three chaplains: a Catholic, a Protestant, and a Mormon. The Catholic priest was supplied from the diocese of Christchurch, who cycled them through for 1-month tours during the summer only. Most of these guys were former missionaries to the South Sea islanders; McMurdo was hardship duty.

Most of the residents of McMurdo, especially the military personnel and the lower-level technicians, had no use for religion. More often than not they seemed openly hostile, in the manner of adolescents the world over. (Up to about age 25, most kids still buy the quaint notion that religion and science are competing systems that both promise the answers in no uncertain terms. By the time age and wisdom hits, at about 30, you're beginning to learn that even small ambiguous shadows of the truth are rare, worth treasuring wherever you find them.) I ran into a number of people who reacted that way to me. No sound bite could answer them. All I really could do was say, "Yes I'm a Jesuit, and yes I'm a scientist. It works for me. See if you can figure it out."

Erebus and Terror

B EFORE WE left for the ice, we took 24 hours for a shakedown trip to the slopes of Mt. Erebus.

In 1839 the British sent out the first expedition intended solely for Antarctic exploration. They built two ships specially designed for the rigors of the ice: the *Erebus*, captained by J. Clark Ross, and the *Terror*, captained by Commander F. R. M. Crozier. In 1841, searching for the south magnetic pole, they penetrated pack ice and reached about 71°S; landing on an island, they took possession of the continent for Queen Victoria and named the area Victoria Land.

Continuing further south into what is now known as the Ross Sea, Captain Ross's expedition eventually reached 78°S. At that point they encountered an impenetrable ice barrier of a sort never before seen. The farthest they could go was a volcanic island—Ross Island, the present site of McMurdo Base. The northernmost point of the island, Cape Crozier, is now the site of intensive seal and penguin studies. But the backbone of the island itself are two volcanic peaks: Mt. Terror and Mt. Erebus.

We set off as a string of Ski-Doos—each dragging a Nansen sled behind us piled high with food, equipment, and tents—and headed across the Ross ice shelf, crossing the cleared path that served as a roadway to the runways on the ice, dodging around floes pushed up by the pressure of the frozen ice over the seawater a mere 10 feet below us. We rounded past the cape where the New Zealand camp, Scott Base, is located; their cluster of green military huts stood out against the snow. Soon we were cruising along at maybe 20 miles per hour, in single file, across the ice.

Driving a snowmobile in Antarctica is a lot different from bouncing over the fields back in Michigan. These machines were big, heavy, and incredibly sturdy; they were also an incredible pain to steer, calling on muscle power that my sedentary lifestyle had allowed to lapse. You held onto a pair of handlebars and controlled the throttle with your right thumb. There was a brake; I don't recall ever using it because, like a boat, the Ski-Doo would slow to a stop almost instantly once the pressure was taken off the throttle.

Starting the machines was an adventure itself. The electric starter worked best only after the engine was warm; first thing in the morning, you'd be better off using the pull rope instead.

There was also a "kill switch" on the dash. That caused many early morning headaches . . . after a dozen futile tries at starting my machine, I'd look up for help, and John Schutt would walk over, flip off the kill switch that I'd accidentally engaged without noticing it, and give me a really dirty look.

In the morning, I'd want to warm up the engine before engaging it; it also helped to run the belts and let them warm up before putting stress on them. Then I'd rock the beast back and forth with all my weight to break whatever ice might be freezing the drive track to the ground, twist the forward steering ski back and forth a bit, then engage the gear, give 'er the gun, and hope that I didn't take off too fast and suddenly drive straight through somebody's tent.

Driving the machines was probably the hardest work we had, day in and day out. It wasn't a simple matter of straddling the nice soft seat, hiding down below the windshield, and opening up the throttle. The trouble was, you had to keep a close watch behind you all the time. You had to stay alert, too; another reason not to get too comfortable behind the handlebars. And, finally, for an awful lot of our travel, the surface was so rough that you couldn't stay seated for more than a few seconds anyway without getting your teeth jarred out of your skull.

And sitting still in Antarctica is the fastest way to freeze to death. Literally.

Instead, the proper way to drive a snowmobile is to kneel, or stand, or crouch . . . or all of the above, in constant motion. It really did feel like sailing a dinghy. You'd be facing sideways, for one thing— with our heavy hoods it was impossible to turn around to look behind you, so you faced sideways, and alternately looked forward and then backward. Forward to follow the track of the snowmobile in front of you (and stop suddenly if they had to stop!) and backward to make sure the sled you were dragging was traveling in your path and hadn't tipped over, wasn't sliding faster than you and threatening to overtake you or tangle your tow rope under your tread (just like towing a boat).

And backward, as well, to make sure the guys behind you were still keeping up. If the snowmobile behind you stopped, then you had to stop, too. And then you'd hope the guy in front of you was paying attention and stopping, as well. Nothing was more disconcerting than to have to stop for some problem, only to see the string of snowmobiles in front of you continue on without you, never noticing your absence. No matter how much the lack of privacy drove me nuts, I never really wanted to be all that alone down there.

We drove maybe a couple of hours, dragging our sleds behind us, gradually crawling our way up the side of the mountain. A deep blue sky surrounded Erebus, which stood ever before us and never seemed to get closer. The only cloud was a little cap on the mountain itself. Mount Erebus is a volcano . . . an active one.

"In November of 1979," Ralph related, "an airliner on a tourist excursion managed to fly right into the side of that mountain. Must have been a cloudy day, classic white-out conditions, and they never even saw it. They never knew what hit them."

I remembered my Peace Corps days in Africa, where death was so close to the surface that you just got used to it. Here seemed the opposite. That little mountain? This calm, perfectly clear, innocent winter day? It was hard to imagine anything could possibly be dangerous out here.

"A lot of my colleagues remember that day," Ralph said, "and the horror they lived through."

Up off the ice shelf, we climbed gently sloping ramps of snow until we were on the flank of Erebus itself. Finally Ralph called a halt. We unpacked our sleds and set up the tents.

Scott tents are great inventions. Almost unchanged in design since the turn of the century, they have the advantage of being relatively lightweight, roomy, and easy to set up in a blowing wind. Imagine a four-sided pyramid, with an aluminum pole (one modern advantage) running down from the peak to each corner. The tent (actually two tents, one inside the other, the space between them where the poles live acting as insulation) is rolled up along these poles.

First job is to unroll it, and lay it out on the ground into a large yellow triangle. Traditionally, the tents are set up crosswise to the wind, which allows for wind shifts; but the wind in Antarctica always blows from the pole, so we set them up with the back facing the wind and the doorway facing north, in the lee. This meant that our yellow triangles were oriented with their points facing south, into the wind. The two back poles were spread wide; a rope was tied to the peak; and with a sudden jerk, the tent was pulled upright on its back poles. As it went up, the force of the wind would get under the tent and push it forward onto the front legs (which one had to spread out quickly as the tent went flying up). If we did it right, the wind would do all the work and the pyramid would fix itself into the ice.

Three things then remained to be done. First, the corners were fixed with pegs, and more pegs pounded into the ice or snow for guy wires to hold the whole thing down in case the wind pecked up even more. Second, the outer edge of the tent was covered over with snow and ice to hold it down and prevent the wind from blowing underneath the walls. And finally, the floor of the tent had to be unfolded and placed over the ice inside the tent.

The job Ralph usually gave me—instantly recognizing that I was half a foot shorter, and 25 pounds fatter, than he was—was to set up the floor of the tent. This meant, however, that I had to crawl through the little tunnel into this tent, dressed in all my winter gear (it was cold outside, and inside!) feeling like the Michelin Man, and futz with a floor that was always bigger than the tent itself, never unfolded smoothly, always managed to cover that glove I'd just set down for the moment, and ultimately backed me into a corner that I couldn't get out of. Because it is such an obviously simple job, I'd end up feeling twice as flustered when it didn't work out right. And feeling like an utter fool.

The next morning we boarded our snowmobiles and headed out to a valley of snow on the shore of the Ross ice shelf. There, in a natural hollow, we had the chance to really try out our Ski-Doos and see just what they could do.

John showed us the easy way to drive down into the bowl. Soon he was spinning his snowmobile around, traveling higher and higher up the rim of the crater at a faster and faster speed.

Ralph turned to me, and asked, "Did you ever see that Elvis Presley movie with the Wall of Death?"

I knew the scene. As a death-defying stunt in a carnival, Elvis takes a motorcycle, goes into an area surrounded by a 20-foot high circular wooden wall, and drives the motorcycle up onto the wood, spinning faster and faster as the cycle climbs the wall.

Down we followed, and soon we were spinning ourselves dizzy. John and Ralph were trying out new-model Ski-Doos that were about half the weight of ours, but equally powered, and they were having a blast.

I was nervous as a cat. I never did care for anything powered by two-cycle gasoline engines, in any format. Outboard motors, lawn mowers, go-karts . . . they never worked right for me.

Maybe I was distracted by the memories. Maybe it was the sharp shadows, as we passed from bright sunshine into the shade of the mountain. Maybe I had just gotten dizzy from going in circles too often. But suddenly I realized I was going wrong.

My Ski-Doo wasn't running around the edge of the bowl—it was running up the rim. At the steepest point. And going slower every second. I had visions of the whole machine toppling over on top of me as it stalled out, the two of us rolling down into the bowl, and a helicopter ride back home with several broken limbs. Not what I wanted to do.

But what to do instead? My Ski-Doo, sensing my panic, was beginning to cough and sputter.

Maybe, I thought . . . just maybe . . . if I gave it enough gas it might possibly have enough power to pull itself out of the bowl. So I jammed my thumb against the throttle and prayed.

The engine roared to life.

Heading straight up the side of the bowl, I realized there was no turning back. I really would tip over now if I tried to turn, or stop; I really would stall the engine if I did anything other than hang on. The only way out, was through.

Balance, I told myself. And keep going straight. I kept going straight.

Straight up.

The roar in my ears was no longer just the engine; it was the wind whistling underneath the Ski-Doo. I was airborne.

I let go of the throttle. The engine slowed to an idle. Slowly, carefully, I stood up in my seat, and admired the view from up there. The world turned quiet as it spun below me. One of those big ugly Antarctica seagulls, a skua, flew past . . . er . . . underneath me. The entire plot of *War and Peace* flashed before my eyes. I got that funny feeling you get in your stomach when you realize the brakes in the elevator have failed. And I prepared for impact.

I kept my balance. The Ski-Doo landed straight, and I landed on it. The seat back, a construction of one-inch metal pipe and thick foam padding, caught my rear end and slowed my decent by bending 30 degrees. The shock of impact killed the engine. All was quiet.

Tranquility Base here. The Eagle had landed.

I got off the Ski-Doo to walk off the shock a bit and reassure myself that nothing important was malfunctioning. All my bones seemed intact. I turned back and paced off the path, from where you could see the snowmobile tracks had left the ground to the spot where the crater marked my landing point. Forty feet. No exaggeration. Really.

And the Ski-Doo roared back to life as soon as I got over the shakes and calmed down enough to turn the key. The only thing damaged (besides my meek and mild facade) was my tailbone. It did feel a little sore where it had hit the metal seat.

"The worst will go away in a few weeks," Ralph reassured me. "But it'll probably never go away completely . . ."

Today, 3 years later, it still hurts; more, when I am tired, or less, when other things are on my mind. But once again, Ralph was right. It has never gone away. And it probably never will.

I expect I will always carry with me that little reminder of my experience with Erebus. And terror.

SOUL ON ICE

ITH ANOTHER mighty roar, the C-130 plane took off. The same kind of plane that had taken us down to McMurdo was now taking us away, to the Antarctic Plateau itself. On the trip from New Zealand there had been about 40 of us crowded into our seats; now there were only five (John had gone ahead with the first plane) and the rest of the plane was filled with Ski-Doos and heavy cardboard boxes. We'd spent the last 5 days filling up those boxes and painting the address "Griffin Nunatak" on them; they'd been carried down to the airfield a few days earlier. We just hoped now that they had all gotten on the plane. This was no place to lose your luggage.

In a funny way, it felt good to be on a familiar plane; at least one thing wasn't entirely new. This time it was crewed by the U.S. Navy, not the New Zealand Air Force, but the routine was the same: strapped into uncomfortable seats along the side of the plane, watching the engineers peering out the windows, counting the engines; feeling the roar through our earplugs as the plane rumbled down the ice and leapt into the sky . . . feeling the familiar tilt as we gracefully circled the field and came back in for a landing. And the familiar 2-hour wait, in a little trailer parked out on the ice runway, while they looked over the engines to try to chase down whatever it was that didn't feel quite right to the pilot.

The flight, once we took off again, lasted over an hour and I was sweating the entire time. There have been times enough in my life when I felt like I was flying into the unknown; never was it so literally true. I trusted Ralph and John, I trusted my fellow travelers, I trusted the guys flying the plane (though it occurred to me, this aircraft was probably older than any of these sailors . . . here I was flying on a 30-year-old plane that'd been maintained all those years by teenagers). I knew, though, that I didn't trust myself. Well, all would be clear when we stepped off the plane. I had camped out on the ice before. For one night, anyway. It's the unknown that frightens us. As soon as I knew what it was like, it would no longer be unknown.

Finally, the plane banked around and seemed to be coming in for a landing. Without windows we could only feel, not see, what was going on. "They're probably going to do a drag first," shouted Ralph to the rest of us, over the noise of the engines. I had no idea what he was talking about.

Then the engines became suddenly louder, and we could see the tension rising in the fliers. With a sudden jolt we hit the surface, and bounced and bounced and bounced . . . and the engines got even louder as once more we broke free and climbed back into the safety of the air. Slowly the plane began a bank to the left, and we could feel it coming around for another try.

"They just made a runway for themselves," said Ralph, "so that they have something hard and smooth for when they take off again."

We landed again with a jerk. More bouncing; more noise. Then, finally, we shuddered to a stop. The back of the plane slowly started opening. Ralph waved us toward the front, where a door below the pilot's cockpit popped open. "Stay clear of the engines," he shouted. "They don't dare shut them down while they're out here."

We followed him to the door. At the door, where the engines were even louder, I could see the blur of the turboprop right next to where we had to walk. I swallowed hard, and stepped off the plane.

Into the wind.

The weather at McMurdo had been like a midwinter day in Michigan. The weather on the plateau was like nothing I had ever experienced, or imagined, in my life.

The wind was incredible . . . 30, maybe 40, miles an hour, bucked up by the wash of the props. And 20 below, of course. The fliers loved this kind of weather—it made it easier for them to land and take off. I pulled up my knit ski cap over my mouth, pulled the plastic face mask down over my eyes and cheeks and nose, and felt the wind go right through both.

There was work to be done. I didn't know if I'd be capable of doing any of it, but at least it kept me moving. The snowmobiles and the boxes of equipment were all on metal pallets; the crew of the plane would push them down the back hatch, then rev the plane up, and move it up and out from under them. Our job was to get the snow-mobiles moving, drag the stuff out of the way, find the tents and the food and the things we needed immediately. I felt lost, hopeless, unable to hear instructions or think for myself from the shock of the cold and the noise of the wind.

"Tent," shouted Ralph over the roar. Somehow, we—he—got it up and staked out. I crawled in and spread out the floor, put down the rubber mats, carried in the boxes with the kitchen gear, and dragged in the sleeping bags. Outside, Ralph pounded in stakes and piled snow up against the base of the tent. Inside, I was still incredibly cold, but at least I was out of the wind.

Fear of the unknown? I now knew what the Antarctic plateau was like. It was no longer unknown. And it scared the hell out of me.

Somehow, the tent got up and the goods got moved around to the right places at the right times. I know I did less than my share of the work. I don't know how my fellow novices on the ice coped, for I was too busy coping myself. The camp was for only one night, but it still had to be set up right. Stoves had to be lit; snow had to be gathered to melt for drinking water; hot chocolate had to be made and drunk. In the midst of it all, the plane had taken off and left us behind. I hadn't even noticed.

There was so much to do, so much to see; good thing the sun never set. It was our first evening, finally, of "the real thing" and I fell asleep early, exhausted by it all.

The story of my life has always been, "nobody tells me anything . . ." and that's how I felt all the next day. I never did hear exactly what our plans were, when we were leaving, where we'd be going. I was just following orders . . . filling the gas tanks of the Ski-Doos was my personal job, which meant driving one of them all over the camp, chasing after wherever all the other guys had parked their own machines, as they were constantly using them to drag boxes about.

It kept us busy all morning. Lunch was a hot meal, well earned. And then, the most wrenching moment, when the nice warm tent that had so protected us from the cold, the place where we could eat and sleep and just go to catch a breath, our refuge and safety . . . was pulled down. Rolled up. Packed on top of the sled. We were naked again. It was time to move. John led the way; I followed, second. I didn't want to have him out of my sight, and I didn't want to be left behind.

I looked back at the line forming, single-file, behind us. Each snowmobile pulled two or three long wooden sleds packed with boxes of food and equipment, wrapped in canvas and rope. The bright yellow rolled-up tents atop the sleds added a rare touch of color. Beyond was Griffin Nunatak, poking up through the ice cap. The blowing snow had already erased all evidence of our camp.

In front of us, my inexperienced eyes could only see a blank, featureless white plain stretching out without relief to an infinite horizon under a piercing blue sky. The emptiness was stunning. In this hollow land the wind blew through my parka, and through my soul. How John could possibly find a path was a mystery to me.

The terrain was rugged. Snow, especially snow that's been frozen for 10,000 years, when bounced over on a Ski-Doo at 20 miles an hour, is not soft. The prevailing winds, from the south, carved it into *sastrugi,* hard snow ridges a foot or so high running north and south for miles. (The word is Russian, I think.) As we rode over them, the sleds bucked and weaved behind us. I worked hard to keep an eye on John, scouting the path before us. We were traveling through crevasse country; indeed, this was possibly the most dangerous part of the whole season right at the beginning. A couple of times he'd stop, test a route, and change his mind. We could not see what he could see; we could only trust him.

His job was not only to find a safe path, but a relatively flat one. The sleds in the rear tipped over once; another time, bouncing down through a shallow ravine, the heavily loaded sled with two barrels of Ski-Doo gasoline broke a runner. John and Ralph wrapped it with rope and went on.

I had no idea how long it would take; maybe 2 hours, I thought. I had overheard "40 kilometers" and I had figured that on our first trip we'd been able to get the Ski-Doos moving at more than 20 miles an hour, according to the little speedometer on the dash. Or was that kilometers per hour? Still, 2 hours ought to do it.

Soon I was cold, but not where I expected it. The Ski-Doo windshield and the face mask actually did a pretty good job of keeping the wind off my body. And my feet, amazingly, stayed warm.

I was trying out some chemical feet warmers that I'd bought up in Marquette (visiting my brother Ed in northern Michigan that last September). Expose these little pads to the air, said the package, and you'd get heat for four hours. Just make sure that there was a way for air to circulate, or you might burn yourself, it warned. There were two kinds . . . smaller ones for feet (where, presumably, your boots kept you insulated) and bigger ones for your hands. Fearing burned feet, I hesitantly tried the smaller ones. For this trip, they seemed to be working. My feet did not burn; in fact, they didn't even feel warm—I couldn't feel the pads at all. But my feet, at least, did not feel cold. (Later on, during the worst days, I'd stuff the hand warmers down into the toes and get a slight feeling of warmth.)

I wore big white "bunny boots" made of a soft plastic that stuck well to ice, in two layers with an air space between. They even had a valve to open when flying in a C-130, so that you could equalize the pressure and keep the boots from exploding . . . giving me pictures of Bozo the clown with his inflatable shoes. But they worked.

After 2 hours, we stopped for a breather. It was hard work, driving the Ski-Doos. Hard on the arms and legs and back. But mostly, hard on the right thumb.

It's the thumb that controls the throttle; let go, and the Ski-Doo stops. But that means, it's the thumb that's doing work nonstop for hours at a time. And no matter how thick your mittens, even with liner gloves underneath they're never thick enough to stop your thumb from freezing.

(Antarctic legend tells of the guy who outsmarted the system. He strapped the throttle tight against the handlebars with duct tape. Then he started up his engine. With a roar, the snowmobile took off at full throttle, throwing him from his seat, and headed in a straight line at top speed across the wide Antarctic ice plateau . . . They called a plane in from McMurdo, the next day, to try to recover it; but it was never to be seen again.)

After 3 hours there was still no end in sight. Around us the ground was featureless, white. Soon I was in a daze, a zone. I started playing favorite record albums in my head . . . humming along as the entire two sides of Abbey Road played on in my memory. Including the scratch that always drove me nuts. I was in Boston again, a student. I was in Chicago . . . I was in San Diego, on the beach with Lynn and Rick. I was anywhere but Antarctica.

John pulled to a stop. I glanced at my watch. Four hours. "Take another break," he told us. We nibbled on chocolate, drank once-hot water from a thermos bottle. Stretched our legs, massaged our thumbs.

Five hours. Would we have time to set up camp, once we'd arrived, before sunset? For some reason I thought that was a really funny joke. It kept me laughing for another 15 minutes at least.

Six hours. Then we came over a crest and saw . . .

It looked like the deepest, bluest lake I had ever seen in my life. The white snow ran down to the shore like a coral beach, with the blue beyond so deep and bright it hurt our eyes as it stretched out beyond us, rippled and curved like waves frozen in time. We had arrived. It was beautiful.

At the edge of the ice, John stopped his Ski-Doo, got off, and started waving his arms over his head.

Ralph roared past on his light, black snowmobile. "Drat it!" he shouted, shaking his fist. The rest of us pulled up near him.

"He always gets the first one!" Ralph complained.

There, at John's feet, was a small black rock.

THE EASTER EGG HUNT

BY THE time we fell asleep that night, there were three more meteorites found within walking distance of camp. We marked them all with red flags on tall thin bamboo poles stuffed in holes chopped into the ice. Up to now we'd left them where we'd found them. In the morning, we'd get our first lessons in how to collect our Easter eggs.

The technique was a little more complicated than you might think. The whole glory of the Antarctic meteorites was the fact that they'd been sitting in nothing but frozen water for 10,000 years; our goal was to make sure we didn't waste all that cleanliness by contaminating them at the last minute.

And it wasn't just fingerprints. Certainly the life-on-Mars controversy had sharpened everyone's awareness of the dangers of contamination by organic chemicals. However, when I visited the curation laboratory at the Johnson Space Center, they made me leave my MIT ring at the door. Worried about brass rat droppings? It turns out that trace metals (as can be found in gold jewelry, for instance) can also upset the delicate isotopic ratios that people like Sara made a career out of measuring.

So only three things were allowed to touch the samples. Snow and ice was okay—sometimes we used a piece of ice to move a sample around, in order to get a better look at it while waiting for the collection kit to arrive. We actually picked up the meteorites with carefully sterilized scissors and tongs that came to us, sealed in plastic, from the Johnson Space Center. But the only other stuff to touch the rocks were the sterilized nylon bags that held them, once we'd picked them up.

Scissors worked much better than tongs for grabbing meteorites, as it turned out. You could use them to dig the rock out of the ice; you could get a tighter grip on the sample with them; and they were handy for cutting open new bags of sterile bags, new bags of number tags, and the long strips of Teflon tape we used to seal the bags shut.

Ralph showed us the procedure. "Everybody gather round," he called, waving us over to the first sample. "It's best if you crouch down and block the wind behind the person who's doing the collecting."

"Who's got the collection kit?" he asked. Laurie brought a small day pack over to him. "Fine," said Ralph. "It's best to do these things in a routine, so you do the right thing out of force of habit. I like to set the pack down in front of me, like this, the top facing towards me. That way I know the measure is in the left pocket, the tape is in the right pocket, the bags are in the middle."

He unzipped the pack, and brought out the scissors and a clear nylon bag.

"The first thing is to see what we've got." He picked up the meteorite with the scissors and held it close, to get a good look at the meteorite's color and texture. "And when you lean over to pick it up, make sure your nose doesn't drip on it," he muttered to himself.

He took a good look, then turned toward John, standing nearby. "O.C.," he called out. "Ordinary chondrite."

John took notes in a small black notebook, recording the data as Ralph spoke.

"About 30 percent fusion crust. Everybody here knows how to recognize fusion crust? It's easy on this one, but sometimes on more weathered samples we get into an argument about whether all black surfaces really are fusion crust.

"Next . . . Sara?" From the side pocket of the collection kit bag, Sara, the old hand, pulled out an oblong metal box. There were numbers visible on one side, and looking closer I could see little wheels attached to each digit; by spinning the wheels, you could dial up any six-digit number. I'd seen these before, hundreds of times, in photographs of lunar rocks; for the first time, I saw one in the flesh.

"Do we assign each rock a number now?" I asked, "and take its picture?"

"We used to photograph them all," Ralph replied. "But no one ever looked at the pictures. Now we just do it for the more interesting ones."

"One and a half," Sara called out, "by one, by one." Peering towards her, over René's shoulder, I could just see her holding the number box up close to the rock. Along the bottom, I realized, were markings in centimeters. She was using it merely for measuring the rock's size.

"Now, we put the rock in the bag." But that was harder than it sounded. I normally have a hard enough time opening up plastic bags in my kitchen back home; out in the ice, with mittens on, it was impossible. But I looked again, and Ralph wasn't wearing gloves or mittens.

He saw my look, and explained, "I'm kneeling on my gloves. The ice is a big cold sink, it stays around 40 below winter or summer, and that goes right through your pants if you try to sit or kneel on it without extra padding. And I need a bare hand to open up the bags; I let my fingers freeze to the outside of the bag, and then when I slide them apart the bag twists open. Like this."

He plopped the little black rock into the bag. "And don't touch the inside of the bag. Now, the rock's at the bottom; we fold it over, once, twice . . . somebody give me a number."

René reached into the right-hand pocket of the day pack and pulled out a plastic bag with little metal tags. "It's either 9011 or 1106.

Let me check . . . the next one is 9012, so I guess 9011 it is." John wrote it down in his book. As the bag with the rock was passed around for us to take a look, Ralph pulled out a black magic marker and wrote 9011 on the pole with the red flag. When the bag reached René, he inserted the metal tag into the last fold and handed it back to Ralph.

"Let's tape it up now," said Ralph. Laurie pulled out the big roll of white tape but after a moment's struggle gave it to Ralph, with his bare hands, to get the roll started. "We always leave a loop for the next time," he warned us. "Otherwise you have to pry it up with your fingernails, which you do not want to have to do in the cold. Anyone who loses the end of the tape gets the bonehead award for the day."

Once he finally got the tape started, he wrapped the bag in it almost completely. "But," he warned us, "Never cover over the metal tag with the tape."

Finally, our little lump of tape and plastic, with a small rock almost invisible inside, was tossed back into the day pack. "At the end of the day, we'll move the samples into the big insulated box on the sled behind John's tent, and do a final count then. It better match the count in John's book."

I remembered that insulated box; it was the one we used to pack the liquor supply. (We each had gotten navy ration cards to buy one week's supply, for which we needed real money—it wasn't supplied by our National Science Foundation grant.)

Something about all this data taking puzzled me. "Since we have the samples anyway," I asked, "why does John bother recording stuff like size and fusion crust out here in the cold?"

"Sometimes NASA screws up," said Ralph, giving René (who worked at NASA/JSC Houston) a dirty look that went unacknowledged, "and gives us duplicate numbers. This way we know that the small rock with 30 percent fusion crust is the 9011 we picked up here, and the big Mars Rock that we're going to find next week, that will also have a tag with the number 9011, was found over in Meteorite Hills. Or wherever."

We went to the next meteorite, and the collection process continued. Every now and then we'd find a rock that was dark black, inside and out: a probable carbonaceous chondrite. And occasionally, the rock would have a lighter color, and a texture more like a collection of basalt fragments: achondrites. But 90 percent of the time, the call would be the same. "O.C.," Ralph would say. Ordinary chondrite.

One night I turned it into a song:

The Ordinary Chondrite Anthem

O.C., can you say? That dark speck on blue ice
that so proudly we seek by sastrugi so gleaming:
a black fusion crust shell, from its perilous flight
o'er the pinnacles crashed, left the ice there still steaming.
And the PI's harsh glare, and John Schutt's steely stare
made us go out and see if the stone was still there.
O.C., we'd not have found you in any other place
than this land where we freeze, seeking stones thrown from space.

I found out about the purpose of the flags later. They stayed up until John had his global positioning satellite (GPS) system working. Then he went to each flag, recorded its position using a hand-held GPS receiver that ran off the cigarette lighter in the Ski-Doo (who'd a thunk?), recording the number on the flag at the same time. Only after he'd gotten back to his tent, downloaded the GPS, and been sure that it had recorded the data properly, did he then let anyone remove the flag. Most of them stayed up for at least the first 3 weeks.

Later that evening I went visiting, peeking into each tent to see how they'd set things up. John, who was short enough to get away with it, had put a big wooden box at the foot of his sleeping bag. One side was a standard U.S. 120-volt (V) electrical outlet. It worked. He had a series of solar cells sitting outside his tent, and a power invertor in the box converted the solar power direct current into 120 volts, 60 cycles alternating current. Not a whole lot of amps, mind you; it wouldn't have powered a toaster-oven or a hair dryer. But it was enough to power his laptop computer and the GPS system.

If you're familiar with GPSs, then you probably know that this system was developed by the U.S. military. They'd launched a series of satellites in orbit around the world broadcasting signals, received by miniature hand-held devices that can use these signals to determine the latitude and longitude of the device to a pretty high accuracy. The military devices, which use a secret decoder chip (sounds like something you'd find in a cereal box, doesn't it?), can give your position instantly to within a couple of feet. Civilian devices don't have the chip, but they can still read out a position good to a couple of yards.

Of course, we wanted positions accurate to centimeters. How do you do it? With something called differential GPS. With two devices, one can measure the relative position of one from the other to within a few centimeters. In fact, we had three; one each on the Ski-Doos used by John and Ralph and one back at camp. To take a reading at the precision we needed meant waiting for 4 minutes while each instrument captured the time and position of five different satellites. At the end of each day, John would download both the mobile GPS units and the camp one into his little computer, and—if they all got good data—the positions of the meteorites he'd recorded that morning would pop out. If he didn't have good data, it meant going back, finding the poles, and remeasuring positions.

Waiting around for 5 or 10 minutes for the GPS to find and lock onto its satellites was a pain; standing around doing nothing is even more boring when it's cold. It was, however, better than the old days, when every position had to be measured with transits and surveyor's poles.

The hope was that, eventually, out of all this positional data a pattern might be seen in which meteorites are found where. So far, with 20 years of data to work with, no such pattern has been found. Even that is probably significant . . . if only we could figure out why.

Within 2 days we were old hands at collecting meteorites. The weather stayed good, clear and blue and not too windy. The regions we searched first included areas that had been picked over briefly 10 years earlier, but they hadn't searched as thoroughly or as systematically as we did now. They left a lot of little stones behind.

We'd make a line of six snowmobiles. Ralph took one end, John took the other, and the rest of us spaced ourselves between them. The two end men set our path and speed; our line became sort of like a sagging "U" as the ones in the middle deliberately traveled just a little behind. This formation made it easier for the ones in the middle to keep track of the leaders on the ends, and helped create an overlap in case any searcher had passed by a meteorite.

There were several Rule Ones, of course. Each meteorite found, was found by all of us; there was no count kept of who got how many, and likewise no "poaching" of meteorites you might see in someone else's path (at least, not until they passed them).

As soon as you found a meteorite, you'd drive up to it, stop, and wave your arms over your head. The rest of us would drop an ice pick or similar object where we were, turn around, and head over to the meteorite that was found. Driving over there, you were careful to always approach from the direction already covered, acting as a second searcher on common ground. It was surprising how often one person's eye would be drawn to a major meteorite far ahead, and thus miss a smaller one in the path on the way to the bigger guy.

After a while, each collector developed his or her own personality, his or her own style. Hearing Sara's English accent, calling out "one-and-a-half" over and over again, inspired us to give her lessons in how to talk American. She progressed successfully through a number of movie formulas, from "I can' stan' it!" (*Singing in the Rain*) to "You lookin' at me?" (*Taxi Driver*). Soon she was fluent in every American dialect, from coast to coast (or, at least, from Flushing Bay to the Hudson River).

Laurie was fussy and meticulous in taping up the meteorites. When there was a job to be done, René rushed to be there first (and then gave the rest of us dirty looks for being slackers); he declared himself "Mr. Krusty," the official estimator of the amount of fusion crust on the rock. John was a man of few words; often, none. When, without warning, he would jump on his Ski-Doo and drive off at high speed in a certain direction, Ralph would translate: "That's John-speak for, 'Okay, enough standing around, what are you guys waiting for? I'm going to head over in this direction. Let's get back to work . . .' "

Though we all had the same standard-issue red suits, we could recognize each other at a glance.

John and Ralph had their own private jackets. Ralph's was a snazzy red-and-black job; John's was blue, and looked like it had seen service with Scott in 1912. (Rumor also had it that it had never been washed; John had a tile of deodorant that he wore on a string around his neck to keep the smell down.)

René had a green scarf. Sara could be identified by her oversized mittens and red flannel hat. My red gaiters made me stand out from the crowd. And Laurie's wind mask was taped over with duct tape. She'd given up on another piece of face-wear: a small knitted "hat" that fit over her nose, held on by a couple of strips of yarn tied behind her head . . . crocheted by her mother in Arizona who has a strange sense of humor.

Every snowmobile bore a picture of our "patron saint," a cartoon emblem of Homer Simpson. (And Ralph had dubbed one of the snazzy black Ski-Doos "Plow King," after a Simpson's episode where Homer got a snowplowing job.) Anyone who's felt like a klutz for days on end, which is what happens when you're wearing too many layers of clothes and your hands are encased in mittens, soon comes to relate naturally with Homer, the hapless nuclear reactor operator who stumbles his way through a weekly animated TV show. D'oh!

As the days wore on, we began to go farther and farther afield looking for meteorites. One afternoon found us well to the northwest, in a region of ice hills, where forces under our feet had pushed the blue ice into a weird conglomeration of 5-foot-high sugar loafs and 3-foot-wide crevasses. The cracks were easy to spot; they were filled with snow, and stood out as rough white stripes crisscrossing the blue ground.

And the snow in them was only a few inches thick. More than once I stopped, making sure the snowmobile was securely on the ice, only to step off into a foot-wide crevasse and sink in up to my knee. Fortunately, no legs were broken; but it was embarrassing at best, scary at worst, and always a shock.

Some of the crevasses were wider than a snowmobile. In such cases, we'd detour to find a narrower spot to cross, or take John's assurances that it was safe to drive over. I could never tell the difference just from looking, but he could.

Our first time in the ice hills, Laurie approached one of those wide crevasses as we gathered to collect a meteorite. Finding herself on the wrong side, she stopped her 300-pound machine and gingerly walked across on foot.

"Good thinking," said John. "How much do you weigh?"

"With all this gear?" she answered. "It feels like a ton, but probably 150 pounds."

"And when you walk, all of that weight is on one foot, maybe half a square foot across. That's about two pounds per square inch. The snowmobile weighs 400 pounds, with you on it, but its tread is about 12 square feet (ft^2). You figure it out."

Laurie, Cal Tech Ph.D. 1994, replied, "About a quarter pound per square inch. Hmm . . ." After that, all of us stayed on our machines when crossing the crevasses.

Finally, one afternoon found us well to the north of the camp, at the boundary of the blue ice field.

"Everyone get off your machines and search on foot," Ralph instructed us. "The wind is always from the south, so little meteorites get blown this way. They tend to gather along the edge here, where the surface is still flat but now it's frost-covered and rough."

Tiny meteorites, less than a centimeter across . . . but we found half a dozen in the next 10 minutes. John even found one buried in the snow, visible only as a dark shady spot until he dug it out.

It was getting close to the end of the day, and the sun was beginning to fade. Indeed, looking up, I saw that the blue sky had gone. In its place, an ever-thickening cloud cover was gathering. "Not a white-out yet," said Ralph, "but we should be heading back, soon." It was a 2-mile drive back to the camp. "Let's collect these, and then get moving."

WALKING IN HEAVEN

HE NEXT morning, I
woke up and something seemed strange. I held the wristwatch up to
my eye; but I couldn't read it. (I wore my watch on my wrist all night,
to keep it warm.) Strange; its fancy dial used to glow in the dark all
night long, but now I couldn't see a thing. In the dark. Oh. Yeah. I
pushed the black sleep mask up off my eyes and peered into the 24-
hour yellow glow of our Scott tents. Quarter to seven, said my watch.

Something seemed strange.

I rolled over, but Ralph was still asleep. His alarm clock would go
off in 5 minutes, I knew. Its ticking drove me nuts. With a sigh, I
pushed myself a little further out of the sleeping bag, and reached over
to light my stove.

Mornings were the coldest time of the day. As the official weath-
erman I had the records to prove it. I had brought out a meteorology
station from McMurdo, a rather nice little setup loaned to us by the

Navy. The sensors sat on a pole outside the tent; a wire under the tent floor connected them to a little station by the head of my bed. I recorded data every 6 hours, except when we were away from the camp.

Cold. Stove. I'd check the weather soon, but first things first. First came the burning paste, flammable jelly that you squeezed out like toothpaste from a tube onto a pan underneath the stove's burner. I'd light the burning paste with my first match, and let the flame heat up the works. The valve had to be hot enough to vaporize the fuel before it entered the burner, in order for the stove to work properly.

A couple of pumps to pressurize the fuel tank, but not too much; you didn't want to spring a leak, and start a "comet," first thing in the morning. The way to cure a leaky flaming stove was to toss it out the door, trailing fire behind it, before it could blow up its gas tank and set fire to the whole tent. Ralph and I alone had three such "comets" that season; none first thing in the morning, thank God.

A minute or two after lighting the burning paste (long enough, I hoped) I opened the valve and put a match to the nozzle. If a tall smokey yellow flame appeared, you shut down fast; that was raw gasoline, and the stove wasn't hot enough. But I saw a woefully tiny blue flame, with a satisfying hiss; all was well. In half an hour, the tent would be comfortable. Till then . . .

I opened the kettle, poured in water that I'd kept in a thermos bottle so it stayed unfrozen overnight, added some chips of ice, and placed it on my stove. In about 10 minutes, it'd make oatmeal and Tang and hot chocolate.

The incessant ticking of Ralph's alarm clock suddenly changed into a harsh ringing. He groaned and cursed and slammed it shut. Ralph is not a morning person.

"Good morning," I said, cheerfully. I am.

He muttered a curse under his breath. But it sounded like more than his normal morning grumpiness.

"Do you hear it?" he asked me.

No, I didn't.

That's what sounded so funny. For the first time in a week, the tent was not flapping in the wind.

Looking around me, I also noticed that the yellow light was coming evenly from every direction. How odd.

Quickly I switched on my weather readouts, checked the temperature and the wind speed and direction. It confirmed what my ears told me. No wind.

"It's only 10 below Celsius," I said in some surprise. "That's about 10 above, Fahrenheit. It's never been that warm before."

"I hope you covered your Ski-Doo last night," said Ralph.

"Why?"

"It's snowing."

I unwrapped the cord holding the inner door closed, crawled through the tunnel to the outer door, opened it up, and looked outside. Ralph was right.

My first blush of excitement over the snowfall—at heart, I'm still a 10-year-old—was tempered quickly by a realization of just what it meant for our work. Simply put, if the ground everywhere was covered with a couple inches of snow, the meteorites would be covered, too. How could we ever find them?

We had camped on a tongue of snow extending into the regions of blue ice. The wind normally came from the south, and in doing so it had formed the snow into long ridges of sastrugi. In the sunshine, it was easy to pick your footing across these ridges; on a Ski-Doo it was rougher, since the snow was frozen pretty hard, but so long as you could see them you could judge your path (and prepare to bounce) accordingly. Like steering a boat on rough water, you either went directly across them or directly into them; hitting at an angle threatened to tip the Ski-Doo over.

All that was fine, so long as you could see the ridges. But in a white out, with no shadows, they became almost completely invisible. Walking was tricky; driving a Ski-Doo was downright dangerous.

It only snowed one day. The wind returned by the next morning, with a vengeance. A good thing, since it was sweeping the blue ice clear; but in the meantime our work outdoors was made even more difficult by drifting, blowing white stuff. The wind-blown snow created a new sound on the tents. The constant rattle of the fabric had added to it the chattering of snow and ice, hitting at 20 miles an hour.

And so the days started a new rhythm.

We'd still wake up at seven, with hope; but the rattle of the wind-blown snow on the tent would give us the bad news. By seven thirty, our morning ablutions complete, Ralph or John would radio in to McMurdo. We'd leave the radio on, just to listen to him and all the other teams of scientists from around the continent with their morning check-ins.

"McMurdo, McMurdo, this is Sierra zero-zero-two, two souls in camp, and a whole lot of penguins; over." That was the Cape Crozier team.

Then would come the geologists in the dry valleys. "Is there a copter available? We were hoping to do a recon over the southern slopes . . ."

"Flight ops will be on at oh-eight-thirty," McMurdo would reply. "We'll pass on your message to them; over."

And one by one the other teams would sign in.

"I'll need to arrange a patch through to Washington, for oh-eight-hundred hours tomorrow morning . . ."

"Tell Henry to bring some fresh batteries. We need C cells and D cells . . ."

And my favorite, a certain group of biologists on one of the islands. Every morning sounded the same. "Uh, yeah. Like, uh, uh, this is, uh, uh, See—, uh, Sierra, uh . . ." We couldn't tell if he was drunk, stoned, or just congenitally out of it. Some people have radio presence; others get stage fright, I guess.

"McMurdo, McMurdo, this is Sierra zero-five-eight." John's voice, transmitting from only 50 feet away, came booming through the loudspeaker. "Six souls on board, and all is well. Overcast, wind-blown snow."

"Sorry to hear that, Johnny."

"Yeah, sounds like another tent day."

"Ralph, are you listening in?" asked McMurdo.

"That's a Roger," said Ralph into the microphone.

"Your DVs are still scheduled for the fourth. They'll be coming by helicopter. But cheer up; they will be bringing mail and resupply; we've scrounged up another case of AA cells for you . . ."

Nine o'clock was normally our time for gathering in front of John's tent to hear the day's plans. But on these snowy days, John and Ralph would meet alone, in John's tent. After, Ralph would walk over to the women's tent, explain what was happening, then come back to ours. I usually got no more than a brief digest. If I'd ask for details, Ralph would get this "didn't I just explain this twice, first to John and René, and then to Laurie and Sara?" look.

Nobody told me anything. It was the complaint of my life. I couldn't even tag along with Ralph to find out first hand what was going to be going on; leaving the tent unoccupied meant turning off the stoves.

So I had to get my revenge in subtle ways.

I made myself even more cheerful every morning; I knew it drove Ralph nuts. With Sara and Laurie and René, we played several games of Monopoly; I always played conservatively, never drawing attention to myself, and usually winning or coming in second. Ralph's big game was cribbage; I made sure to never learn how to play. And everyone in the camp came down with a horrible cold; everyone, that is, but me. Ralph suffered terribly for 2 weeks. Revenge, though private, was sweet.

Pleasant it was; but in the long run, there was no profit to be had by playing mind games with someone you were trapped in a tent with for weeks and weeks. Especially someone as equally skilled at it as Ralph.

He had a thick book with him, *Best Science Fiction Stories of 1995,* and he thoughtfully shared with me the plot twists of each story while he read them. His copies of *Sports Illustrated,* on the other hand, he shared with the women's tent and then John and René. I never got to see them.

In a word, by the end of a week trapped in the same tent, Ralph and I were driving each other nuts. The trouble was, of course, that there was no escape. We were 200 kilometers from anywhere, but we were never alone.

The snow kept us camp-bound for 12 days straight. And it wasn't the only thing that kept us from looking for meteorites. Even before the snow, we'd lost a couple of days just to necessary camp chores.

The month before we arrived, John and Ralph had arranged for Henry, the Twin Otter pilot, to leave a fuel dump near where we'd be camping. It did feel strange to be off in the utter middle of nowhere and come across a pile of boxes and barrels. The barrels held Ski-Doo gas; the boxes had bottles of oil and cans of Coleman fuel. It all had to be dragged back to camp, a distance of probably a couple of miles. Not so long as to be impossible; long enough to take a good chunk of the day, though.

The standard technique for getting the barrels of fuel to our place was to tie a rope around each one and drag it over the ice behind a Ski-Doo. It sounded pretty dangerous to me, but I figured Ralph knew what he was doing. Halfway back to camp, my barrel managed to get itself untied. Turning back to retrieve it, I noticed it had sprung a leak.

I wasn't the only one it happened to. Seems they'd switched to a different type of barrel, made of thinner steel. Ralph described the situation in a few colorful words, repeated several times at various volume levels. Not only did it mean we'd have to use a sled to carry the rest of the barrels back—the sled that had been broken during our traverse from Griffin—but it also meant calling in the environmental cleanup squad from McMurdo. Antarctica is a pristine continent, and every kind of spill had to be reported, cleaned up, and described on endless paperwork back at civilization. Not to mention the loss of the fuel itself. And waiting for the cleanup crew to fly out, in Henry's Twin Otter, meant another workday lost.

For me, however, it was the first I would get to see of Henry the Swiss pilot and his twin-engined Otter. It truly was amazing the places he could go, and land, with that airplane. A typical wind on the plateau blew at about half his cruising speed to begin with; coming in to land, into the wind, he almost looked like he was hovering. Likewise, the distance he needed to take off was negligible; I'd flown Ski-Doos farther than that!

I was eager to see how he landed his plane; so, naturally, the first time he came Ralph asked me to stay inside the tent and stand by the radio.

"He'll announce himself by his radio call sign, which are the letters KBG," Ralph explained. "We'll also be listening on portable radios, but I'd like you to be backup in case they don't work. So if you hear 'KBG' calling for 'Sierra zero-five-eight,' that's him looking for us. Take the message, or come get us."

"You say the KGB is coming after us?" I asked.

"K-B-G," said Ralph, disgustedly. He gave me a dirty look and left the tent.

The snow meant even more work for us. Blowing winds created tall drifts between the tents. Worse, they had buried six of our sleds in several feet of snow, and we needed to get at them. We also needed to dig them free of the drifts before the snow hardened; we were going to need those sleds when we broke camp at the end of the season.

So one day, Ralph and John discovered some important work to be done elsewhere, and assigned the four of us to dig out the sleds. As usual, René put himself in charge; since he was always in the tent with John and Ralph when they discussed the day's plans, he was often the only one who had any idea of what was going on. He gathered up the shovels and directed us to start digging at the sled buried the deepest in the snow.

Four people swinging shovels pretty much filled up all the available space around that sled. I stuck in my shovel, dug out a pile of snow; and again; and again. By the fourth shovel full, I was feeling dizzy. And there was a long way to go.

I fell back to catch my breath; René gave me a dirty look, and started digging huge gulps of snow out of the area that I'd barely scratched. On the other side of the sled, Sara and Laurie were churning away like twin steam shovels. Panting, I contemplated the situation.

I looked around, and saw the other 13 sleds; half of them also needed serious digging out. This would take forever, and probably give me a coronary attack. On the other hand . . .

Hard work, I decided, is a sign that you haven't thought through the problem carefully enough.

I walked over to my Ski-Doo, grabbed a tow rope, and drove to a sled far away from the other people. I wanted no witnesses if this didn't work.

I dug out the front of the sled enough to find a place to tie the tow rope on. I went along the side of the sled on each side, dug a hole down to the runner, stuck the shovel under the runner, and pried it up ever so slightly, breaking the bond freezing it to the snow. Then I powered up the Ski-Doo, put it in low gear, and jammed on the gas. Rocking back and forth, like I did all the time driving in Michigan winters, I managed to make a bit of a path in front of the sled. After three or four jerks with the Ski-Doo, the sled suddenly pulled free of the drift.

I towed it over to a flat, snow-free piece of ice, then went off looking for the next sled to conquer.

Five sleds later, I drove back to the one the other guys had been working on all this time. "Ready to pull it out?" I asked.

René gave me a slow burn worthy of Oliver Hardy.

I tied the Ski-Doo to the front of their sled and gently eased on the gas. The sled slipped quietly out of its nest of snow.

Once again, René only glared.

Looking over the rest of the camp, I commented, "That seems to be all six. How about a coffee break?"

René muttered something. Laurie and Sara invited me over to their tent, and I scalded my mouth on some of Sara's darjeeling.

When Ralph returned, he nodded, but made no comment. Next morning, however, still too blowy to work, he suggested a new task.

"The fuel barrels," René announced to us. "Ralph wants us to refill all the gas cans . . ." A normal job, necessary and never ending. "But first, we'll have to get at the barrels that are buried in the drifts."

We had dragged about six 55-gallon drums of gasoline over to a spot north of the camp, downwind, and the blowing snow had all but covered them. Around them the snow was three feet deep and hard as a rock. Our job would be to pull those drums out of their hole and onto the hard snow so we could get at them.

Each drum weighed about 300 pounds. Ralph could wrestle them, single-handed; none of us could.

Silently, shovels in hand, the four of us stood around the half-buried drums. René, with a sigh, started digging toward one end, and the rest of us joined in. Soon we had a space around the drums cleared out, but the drums themselves were still three feet below the surface where we wanted them.

"Ralph could just pick one up and carry it out, I suppose . . ." I suggested. René gave me yet another dirty look.

"Stand back," he said. With a couple of swift shovels, he'd cleared a ramp down into the hole.

"I suppose we could try rolling them out?" I suggested, tentatively. René just ignored me.

Instead, he walked over to my Ski-Doo, grabbed the tow rope, and wrapped it around the first barrel. He attached the other end to the back of the Ski-Doo, powered it up, and in about 30 seconds had dragged the barrel up his ramp and out of the hole.

This time he gave me another look, half triumph and half amusement. "Two can play that game," it said.

In half an hour we had cleared the hole.

And still the days wore on. To give himself exercise, and an excuse to get out of the tent, Ralph would go ice skating in the evenings. Up and down the ripply blue ice, for a hundred yards in either direction. It was tricky, he pointed out; the ice was rough, and unlike any ice rink back home it went uphill and down.

At his suggestion, I went out myself for walks. I always kept within eyesight of the camp, of course; but you didn't have to be too far away to feel very alone. It was a precious feeling.

"Take your Walkman," Ralph suggested. It was a great idea. A friend of mine in Chicago, Judy Thompson, had put together a tape of atmospheric classical music . . . Russian Orthodox psalms by Stravinsky and an "Agnus Dei" set to the tune of Barber's "Adagio for Strings." It was the perfect sound track.

One afternoon, in near white-out conditions, I was stepping slowly and carefully to the haunting Barber melody. All was white and slow and peaceful, all around me. I recalled a story Ralph had told me . . . once, while giving an Antarctica slide show back in Cleveland, a little-old-lady had come up to him and said, "You've been to heaven." Ralph was taken aback. But she explained. "I dreamt about heaven last night," she told him. "And it looked just like your pictures." Ralph, the skeptic, could only nod in agreement. And walking out there wrapped in whiteness, I knew just what she meant.

The sun was just a dot of light in a white sky; the ground and the sky met without changing shade or color. Everything around me, up and down, looked the same. It felt like being suspended in a cloud, stretching on as far as the eye . . .

My eye stopped with a jerk. There was something black, ahead of me. Yes . . . another meteorite! A big one at that.

But how would I ever find it again?

I looked back to the camp, just barely visible behind me; and walking as straight a path as I could, I headed back and grabbed a flag and an ice-chipper. Then I retraced my steps. Fortunately, parts of the ice were still covered in soft snow; I could make out my fresh footprints. Eventually, I found the rock again and planted my flag.

WE'VE GOT COMPANY

FEW DAYS later we awoke
to a louder wind and a colder cold than I had ever experienced before.
Checking the weather gauge, it read nearly −30°F, with a wind
approaching 40 miles per hour. A quick calculation showed me the
windchill factor outside was a pleasant −77°F.

I scrawled the information on the tattered notepad I kept next to
the weather station. A quick thumbing through it confirmed my suspicion: December 4 was the coldest day we'd had yet.

Meanwhile, Ralph was chatting with the folks at McMurdo.
"That's a Roger," he was saying. "Expecting the copter at 1000 hours.
We'll show the nice folks a good time." Signing off, he nodded my
way. "DVs at ten o'clock."

"Bandits at twelve o'clock high," I muttered to myself. This, I
decided, would be interesting.

The big white helicopter had already made one stop by the time it got to us; its range wasn't enough to reach us without refueling, but there was a base on the way that the DVs—distinguished visitors— had wanted to see. We were dressed to the nines, ready to greet them. I was wearing just about every layer of clothing I'd been issued.

Frankly, the weather was so awful it was almost fun. Just knowing that we wouldn't be driving any Ski-Doos in this howling gale was enough to relieve my mind; I'd never be out of walking distance from a warm tent and hot chocolate.

But there was also delightful arrogance to our stance. A month earlier, this sort of wind would have frightened me to death. This was far colder, and windier, than that first day at Griffin. But my Polartec seemed to be handling it just fine, and I had to admit that −25°F in Antarctica wasn't nearly as bone-chilling as 35°F in Tucson. Somehow, this felt like home.

The helicopter circled around to the south, then came slowly, and noisily, in our direction. It seemed to take forever landing; not like Henry, who'd have been here and gone by now. The DVs were getting the royal treatment.

Ralph described who'd be coming. "First, there's some lawyer from the National Science Foundation (NSF) headquarters in Washington. They put the press office under her, but it's not clear she is here for that reason. She's here mostly for the adventure, I think. That's Ms. Avocado. Next is a Mr. Major; he's the head of the Air Force scientific research group. But he's a civilian." (Yes, I've changed these names . . . I've forgotten their real ones!)

"And finally, of course, our old friend Doctor Zare." Richard Zare, an eminent member of the National Academy of Sciences, had been involved in the life-on-Mars rock; it was his lab that analyzed it for organic compounds. This fact-finding trip would actually be his first trip down here. He and Ralph were on opposite sides of the scientific fight of the century, and compared to Ralph (or any of us) he was a heavyweight.

A videotape of a recent press conference he'd held had been shown to everyone at McMurdo while we were there, I guess so we'd know what he looked like. The impression I had gotten from the tape, and the scuttlebutt at McMurdo, was that he was a spherical idiot: no matter what angle you looked at him, he was an idiot. I was expecting the worst. But Ralph needed a good report from Zare to keep the ANSMET program running.

Finally, with a slowly slowing thwap-thwap-thwap the helicopter settled onto the ice, and two bundled-up Michelin men in red stepped out.

Mr. Major was short and round; he turned into the wind, shuddered, and fell back to the side of the 'copter. Next out was Zare; a much taller man than I had expected, he bounded out and eagerly faced directly into the blast of the wind.

That was two. Where was the third? Finally, stepping out gingerly, came someone dressed as if to go skiing in Colorado. Ms. Avocado obviously preferred her own fashion sense to NSF's. She struck a pose by the helicopter hatch.

"I'd like to introduce . . ." Ralph started in as master of ceremonies. "From my left, that's René Martinez, he's from the Johnson Space Center . . ."

"You're the technician from JSC?" asked Mr. Major.

"Yes . . ." René admitted it, surprised at the eagerness Major's voice.

"Great," said Major. "Can you fix my goggles? I can't see a thing out of them!"

And no wonder. The helicopter had obviously been heated, and humid; stepping from it onto the ice, a layer of frost had grown over everyone's glasses.

"This is Dr. Laurie Leshin, of UCLA," Ralph continued. He emphasized the "doctor;" it was something her friends had learned to do, to overcome one's normal first impression at seeing how youthful and attractive she was.

"Laurie Leshin?" exclaimed Dr. Zare. He reached out his hand and shook hers, vigorously. "I'm so delighted to meet you." Yeah, right, I thought to myself; not merely an idiot, a pompous idiot. But he continued addressing Laurie with great enthusiasm, "I've read your thesis!"

She was speechless.

So was I. A month of my prejudices evaporated in the wind. It was an incredible compliment; it was also a compliment that would be extremely hard to fake.

Ralph finished the introductions, and proceeded on to business. "I thought you might like to see how we collect meteorites. Just a short walk upwind from here, in fact, is a meteorite that Dr. Consolmagno found just the other day; we've left it there until now, so we can collect it in your presence and show you how it's done. And as we go along, feel free to ask any questions. Yes?"

Ms. Avocado spoke up first. "Is there a ladies' room anywhere around here?"

Ralph was stopped in midstream. Her first question was one he couldn't answer.

"Come with me," said Laurie. "You can use our tent, we'll show you how it's done."

After a wait, standing in the wind shuffling our feet, the women returned and our crew finally started on its polarward trek.

John was already ahead of us, having driven a Ski-Doo with a GPS system up to the rock. On the way, Ralph tried to describe our search techniques, but it was obvious that in the wind it would be hard to hear much of what he was saying. We soon split into three small groups, clustered around each of the DVs.

The meteorite was barely a hundred yards upwind of the camp, but even a hundred yards was hard going in that gale. It was clear, too, that walking on ice was a skill extremely tricky for the newbies to master.

Mr. Major spoke up first. "This is nuts," he said to Sara. "What the hell am I doing out here?"

"Would you like to go back to the tent for a cup of tea?" Sara replied.

He turned to her with love and admiration in his eyes. Taking her arm, he turned and let her support him as they walked back to her tent. "Let me tell you about my grandchildren . . ."

Laurie and Zare were engaged in vigorous conversation. He wanted to know everything about us: our work, our camp, our research. He saw my weather station, and asked about typical conditions on the ice. He saw the flags, and wanted to know about John's research into ice motions. He saw the poles set up by René with cosmic ray detectors taped to them at various distances above (and below) the snow level, and so the use of cosmic ray spallation products to date the lifetimes of meteorites had to be explained.

It was clear that Zare's interest and compliments weren't carefully scripted lines; he, like me, was a nerd. He was one of us. And he wouldn't be capable of reading a person well enough to lie to them. I liked that.

We reached the meteorite and in his enthusiasm Zare rushed up to take a closer look. The next moment he had disappeared from sight. I stopped and looked around; then down. He was sprawled on his back, with a sheepish look on his face. As Ralph and Laurie helped him up, I heard a voice beside me. "Oh, dear, it's so slippery. May I take your arm?"

Ms. Avocado demanded my full attention.

"You're the Jesuit, is that right?" I admitted as much. "Good," she said. "I so wanted to talk with you." Well, I thought, this was a group that knew how to say the right things! "I've just joined a church, you see; it's an Episcopal church in Washington."

"The Episcopalians are wonderful people," I said politely.

"I used to be very active in our local Catholic parish," she explained, "but I finally could no longer tolerate the way that women were being systematically excluded from the decision-making processes of the Church . . ."

I looked around me. The sky was a deep, dark blue, with tiny wisps of clouds racing by in the wind. The sunlight was dancing off facets and crevasses in the ice. From here to the horizon was a sheet of rolling, dipping aquamarine. Wind-blown snow whipped past us at 40 miles per hour. We were 200 kilometers from the next human beings, 2000 miles from civilization, 12,000 miles from home.

At least I was. She was still trapped in Washington.

ACQUAINTED WITH ALL MY WAYS

"I AM IN Antarctica," I said to myself. "I have always been here. I will always be here. I will be here forever." It was 4 weeks into our trip. The beginning had become forgotten in the mists of time. The end was nowhere in sight.

"Hey, Guido," called René from the other side of the tent. "You're talking to yourself again."

Some things had changed. The weather had started to clear. One day Henry and his airplane showed up again with two new visitors to our camp: Kim, a journalist from Hawaii, and Andy, a snowmobile technician from McMurdo. They'd be living with us for a week, taking the place of Sara and John who were headed out for a reconnaissance camp in the Meteorite Hills. It meant some shuffling of personnel; Andy took Sara's spot, Kim moved in with Ralph, and I moved over to René's tent.

Every tent had slightly different routines, and it was fun to try out some new ones. For one thing, René and I agreed to share cooking duties. Ralph had done all the cooking when I was tenting with him, and while I appreciated not having to do the work, it was nice, for a change, to have a little more control over what I ate. My spaghetti sauce wasn't too bad; René's Texan Chili was superb. René was a Texan, and proud of it.

We shared music, too. René played bass in a rock band back home (my secret dream) and had lots of insight into popular music. We traded favorite tapes back and forth.

Along with tapes, we traded stories. René was the son of a U.S. diplomat, raised in a series of embassy compounds (and schools) across Latin America. It didn't sound like a life he particularly missed. Of all his stories, the one that amused me most was his description of following the rebellious "sixties" (he was barely in junior high then) by buying "alternative lifestyle" clothing and peace buttons mail order, from the Sears Catalog.

He worked now in the meteorite receiving group at the Johnson Space Center in Houston, and seemed to know just about everyone in the field. I envied him the ease with which he made friends, though his cynicism could get wearing at times.

One thing he was not cynical about was his family. He clearly missed his wife, doted on his daughter Laurel, and he even had nice things to say about the dog who had chewed up his record collection!

In return, I felt I had no stories to give. My tales of life in the field of planetary sciences over the last 20 years cut no ice with him; he knew more of those people than I did. And he showed no interest in anything I had to say about living in Rome—he'd grown up overseas, that was nothing new. My life as a Jesuit held no interest for him; fact was, he was bitterly anti-Catholic (even though he had great things to say about the brothers who taught him at St. Mary's College). I suspected it had something to do with a too-strict upbringing, or growing up overseas; whatever the cause, it left me with little to talk about.

In fact, it struck me as strange that no one on the trip was particularly interested in hearing about my "different" kind of life. Granted, none of the others were particularly religious; I didn't expect to engage anyone in particularly deep theological discussions. But the only one to even ask, "What's it like to live in the Pope's summer home?" was the normally taciturn John. It was as if everyone else felt strangely uncomfortable with the whole topic.

Fact was, I kept my religious life very much to myself. When I moved into René's tent, I brought with me not only my grey bag with my tooth brush and hand cream (dry skin is murder down there), but another tote bag, this one red, that I kept close by my pillow and opened only when no one else was around. It was far too private. It held my Bible, Ordo, prayer book, and a Tupperware container with 50 consecrated hosts.

Opened only when no one else was around? There was no such time! So I invented one. About 2 a.m. every morning, when I knew that René (or Ralph) was asleep, I'd wake myself up and pull out the red bag. I'd say a morning prayer and check the Ordo for the day's scripture readings, looking them up in my tiny-print Bible. And then I'd follow a little set of prayers that Father Joep van Beeck, SJ, my retreat director back in Chicago, had put together for taking the Eucharist outside of the Mass.

Was I being a coward, hiding my religion? Or being discreet? Maybe both.

Many months later, Thaddeus Jones from Vatican Radio asked me about the spiritual side of being in Antarctica. Spiritual? Most of the time I felt grumpy, tired, and stressed!

Still, it was the right question. One aspect of it was the deep humility you learned, comparing yourself and your puny skills against the raw struggle of staying alive in that climate. You recognized that you were utterly dependent upon the people around you; and they, in turn, depended on you in ways you never felt adequate to fulfill. Another side was the breathtaking majesty and beauty of our setting; God is extravagant in His creation.

Another aspect was recognizing that, though faith could be subtle at times, it was no more subtle than the connection between the history of the solar system and a few specks of rock on the Antarctic ice.

Indeed, I realized that most of my life I live day to day, circumscribed in a world not much bigger than home and office and my next meal—a universe not much bigger than three tents and an empty horizon. It wasn't only in Antarctica that I would be liable to think that what I saw before my nose was all there was to see.

Religion, like astronomy, does tell a different story, however. The real world is a lot bigger. And we humans, puny though we seem, are big enough to realize it, accept it, and deal with it.

But mostly I kept coming back to a psalm well known to most Jesuits, a psalm (Psalm 139, vv 1–12) often used at the beginning of our annual spiritual retreats.

> *O LORD, you have searched me and known me.*
> *You know when I sit down and when I rise up; you*
> *   discern my thoughts from far away.*
> *You search out my path and my lying down, and are*
> *   acquainted with all my ways.*
> *Even before a word is on my tongue, O LORD, you know*
> *   it completely.*
> *You hem me in, behind and before, and lay your hand*
> *   upon me.*
> *Such knowledge is too wonderful for me; it is so*
> *   high that I cannot attain it.*
> *Where can I go from your spirit? Or where can I flee*
> *   from your presence?*
> *If I ascend to heaven, you are there; if I make my*
> *   bed in Sheol, you are there.*
> *If I take the wings of the morning and settle at the*
> *   farthest limits of the sea,*
> *even there your hand shall lead me, and your right*
> *   hand shall hold me fast.*
> *If I say, "Surely the darkness shall cover me, and*
> *   the light around me become night,"*
> *even the darkness is not dark to you; the night is*
> *   as bright as the day,*
> *for darkness is as light to you.*

The last lines felt especially appropriate here in the land of the midnight sun.

HUNTING THE
WHITE ELEPHANT

ONE SUNDAY morning about 2 weeks before Christmas, we found ourselves at the finish of a section of blue ice. John and Ralph conferred for a few moments, then decided it was a fine day for a road trip. So we took off, almost on the spur of the moment, for Elephant Moraine.

It was a 20-mile drive on our snowmobiles, but the weather really was perfect; bright, sunny, not too windy, not too cold. We traversed across crevasse-filled ice peaks, playing follow the leader with John, then down into a stunning blue basin of ice surrounded by brilliant white snow hills. Overlooking the basin, we stopped as Ralph gave us instructions.

"So far as we know," he said, "no one has ever searched for meteorites in this ice field. It should be pristine; and, as far as we understand how meteorites get concentrated here, it should be just chock full of meteorites. All we want to do today, however, is a fast recon. So spread out wide, and travel at a good clip. But if you see any meteorites, stop and let us know."

This was no meticulous Easter egg hunt. This was a raid, like a squadron of fighter planes swooping over enemy territory, hunting for targets. With mounting excitement we spread out and roared into the valley.

An hour later, we met together on the other side of the ice lake. Result: zero meteorites. None. Zilch.

"Oh, well," said Ralph, disappointed.

Instead, we carried on toward the moraine itself.

At first it just looked like a dirty hill in the distance. As we got closer, we began to see little spots on the ice. Rocks! Meteorites? Well, no . . . Soon it was hard to steer the Ski-Doo across the ice, for all the rocks on the surface; but they were all terrestrial rocks. Or almost all, anyway.

Ralph stopped and dismounted, and soon we all joined him, walking from rock to rock, looking at each one, looking for meteorites.

"The local rocks are more angular than meteorites," he reminded us, "and they don't have the black fusion crust. And looking closer you'll be able to see . . ."

Well, *he* would be able to see. But I couldn't. I was wearing my contact lenses. At least they didn't fog up under the face mask, but with them in I couldn't focus on anything closer than eight feet away. Even the rocks at my feet were slightly blurry. Bending down to look more closely at any one, all details got washed out into a featureless mush. While everyone else started egg hunting again, I was left feeling frustrated and useless.

After a few minutes, though, John mounted his Ski-Doo and took off. I followed. Rounding the rock-covered hill, we found a true mountain of rocks. He drove his machine right onto the rocks, climbing to the peak, and set his GPS device running to get an accurate reading on the position and height of the moraine. I parked further downhill, and climbed on foot after him.

The view was stunning, and the feeling of walking on rocks again was strange and serene. It had been more than a month since my feet had touched anything but ice.

John and I returned to the group, and together we drove down the hillside to the broad sweep of rocks that made up the rest of the moraine. At the edge of the moraine we traveled again out to the ice, looking rock by rock on the icy surface, searching for meteorites. It just made me feel frustrated all over again.

The others in our group, with younger eyes, had better success. "I think I found a Mars rock!" Ralph exclaimed at one point. "I bet it's a shergottite!" (He was wrong; but still it turned out to be a howardite, which is interesting in its own right.) And, indeed, something about Elephant Moraine brought out the Mars rock fever in us all.

The reason was simple enough. Although ALH84001 had captured all the media attention, it was really another Martian meteorite that had provided our first big breakthrough in understanding that whole class of meteorites: Elephant Moraine (EET) 79001. That was the rock with the tiny bubbles of trapped air that matched almost exactly the atmosphere on Mars. It held the "smoking gun" evidence that said it—and its chemical companions—must indeed have originated on Mars.

We got home late that night, tired but happy. At least we didn't have to worry about getting home before sundown. In fact, driving back, I spent some time just looking up at the Moon and the Sun, both visible overhead, and marveled at how their complicated motions, so strange to my northern-hemisphere eyes, could be so easily explained by the model of a round, spinning Earth.

At least it made sense intellectually. But it made no sense in my gut.

My sense of direction was, in fact, constantly turned around in Antarctica. I was used to thinking of the Sun as sitting in the southern half of the sky. Even though I knew in my head that here in the southern hemisphere the opposite was true, this instinct persisted, so that I constantly confused north and south. Indeed, at some level I would more easily believe that the Sun traveled west to east than to give up this idea that the Sun was in the south. Of course, that made midnight all the more confusing; because then, the Sun really was in the south, and it really did travel west to east.

Adding the Moon to this picture just furthered the confusion. Except when it was closest to the Sun, it would be easily visible to the naked eye. But the Moon's orbit moves it around to mimic the position of the Sun at different times of the year; the full Moon, for instance, sits where the Sun would sit six months later. In other words, a crescent Moon up to three days old would always lie above the horizon in December, just like the Sun; but the full Moon was never visible. (I confirmed these motions when I got back to my computers. But the slight inclination of the Moon's orbit to the ecliptic adds further confusion.) Of course, in retrospect, it made perfect sense. But at the time it was just one more way that I felt disoriented, a stranger in a strange Antarctic land.

NORTHWARD HO!
THE WAGONS

'TWAS THE night before Christmas and across all the ice
not a creature was stirring (not even John's mice).
The kids were all snuggled in down sleeping bags,
all dreaming of space rocks with bright silver tags.

René in his kerchief, Laurie in her nose cap,
John with his poofter tile, Sara's red hat,
Ralph and his ticking clock, and I triple-wrapped,
had just settled down for a short summer's nap

When out on the ice there arose such a clatter
Ralph sprang from his bag to see what was the matter.
Away to the tent door he sprang like a flash
as he cut through the door strings, like to make a pee dash,

When what to his wondering eyes should appear
but a Twin Otter plane! He watched as it drew near.

'Twas flown by a pilot so lively and friendly
that he knew right away: "Why, it must be Saint Henry!"

O'er pinnacles, sastrugi, and blue ice it flew
being pulled by eight objects—each a tiny Ski-Doo!
Past Scott tents and Nansens like comets they came.
He whistled and shouted and called them by name:

"On, Homer! and Homer! and Homer!" he did sing,
"And Homer! and Homer! and Homer! and Plow King!"
To the top of the peaks, almost into a stall—
Then dash away, dash away, dash away all . . .

Henry spoke not a word but went straight to his work
as he flew past each Scott tent then turned, with a jerk,
And by every cruiser tube hole he did fly,
pushing through lots of letters and fresh resupply.

For Laurie, a job letter: hard money, tenure;
plus "Instant Stud Muffins" (add vodka and stir).
For John, a new GPS, scented sublime,
and a trip to a mountain that's never been climbed.

Ralph's gift was a Mars rock delivered by rocket;
Guy's gift was world peace, and a basket of chocolate.

René got guitar strings strung on a new Gibson
and a snapshot of Laurel with her Born-Again boyfriend.
For Sara, a teapot with darjeeling tea,
plus, to shut up her critics, a complete OED.

Then quick as a flash—for he didn't stay long—
the Twin Otter leapt to the air and was gone.
But I heard him exclaim as he flew without fear,
"Merry Christmas—that's a Roger! This is KBG, clear."

—ON THE ICE, CHRISTMAS 1996

We celebrated Christmas on the evening of the 24th of December.
The final meteorites had been collected; after being held up a day for

bad weather, the last reporter (Mary Roach, from *Discover Magazine*) had come and gone; our finds had been inventoried; and our bags and boxes pretty much packed up. It was time for one last party, before saying goodbye to the ice.

Nearly everyone had thought to bring gifts, mostly small joke items like toy penguins and Pez candies. Ralph gave everyone an authentic Hoppalong Cassidy pocket knife, in honor of his retired advisor, Bill Cassidy, the founder of the American ANSMET program. We told stories and jokes and played games. I recited my version of *The Night Before Christmas,* and then described to the rest of the team what living with Ralph had been like . . .

Top ten clues to Ralph's true nature:

10. Various parts of the camp have been marked by yellow splotches.
9. He prefers food that makes its own gravy.
8. He has to turn around at least three times before settling down for the night.
7. Every morning he scratches his back, looking for fleas.
6. When you ask him his name, he answers, "Ralph! Ralph!"
5. He keeps digging holes out in the backyard, when he thinks no one is looking, then covers them up again.
4. His favorite activity is to go out and retrieve various dull, ordinary-looking rocks, which he then brings back to camp and treats like they were treasures.
3. He won't let just anybody rub his tummy.
2. He is loyal, trustworthy, dependable, but his nose is cold (and tends to drip).
1. Don't try to outstare him. He's not called "alpha-Ralph" for nothing . . .

It turned out that I spoke more truthfully than I'd realized. Ralph admitted then that, in fact, he'd been raised on a farm in northern Wisconsin where there were no kids his age for miles, only dogs to play with. We admitted how we thought he made a pretty good pack leader, all in all.

It was a sentimental moment; but not a completely relaxed one. Because we all knew what the day ahead involved.

It was 9 a.m. Christmas morning, and we were up and scurrying around the camp, doing the final packing, tying the boxes onto the Nansen sleds and roping up their canvas sides. It was time to go home.

The weather was cold and blowy, the air filled with wind-blown snow. On any other day we'd have stayed in the tents. But Ralph and John had explained it last night.

"We need a day to get back to Griffin Nunatak," said Ralph. "Another day there, to pack the pallets to be loaded onto the planes. That means if we leave tomorrow, we can get picked up on the 27th."

"That's a Friday," John pointed out.

"Saturday would normally be all right, too, but it's the holiday season. New Year's is going to be celebrated early at Mac-town, so they've declared Saturday a holiday."

"And Sunday is everyone's day off."

"Right," continued Ralph. "So if we don't travel tomorrow, we may as well stay another 2 days, and that means that we'll run into scheduling problems getting flights out of McMurdo after the first. I'm not sure of their schedule, or if the flights from Christchurch will be running on the first of January."

"So if we don't leave tomorrow," John summed it up, "it might mean an extra week down here."

Much as we loved Antarctica, an extra week did not sound all that attractive. So we struggled in the snow and the wind, tying down boxes and dragging the sleds in place.

Taking down the tents themselves, the last item of business, was the most wrenching. No doubt about it . . . as we rolled them up and strapped them to the top of the boxes, there was no looking back. We were really going. Merry Christmas.

"We're taking a different route home," Ralph shouted to us through the wind. "Because of the weather. We decided to avoid the crevasse fields we went through on the way here. It means that it'll take longer, but in some ways it should be easier, especially at the end. The worst part of the trip will be at the beginning. We'll be traveling with the wind coming from the side at first, not behind us. But eventually we will be turning downwind. So keep reminding yourself, it will get better eventually."

We had 14 sleds to divide among six drivers. That meant that a couple of us would be dragging three sleds instead of two. René, as usual, immediately volunteered for the harder duty. I declined, but in a moment of guilt decided that my two sleds should include the largest one of the bunch. Slowly we jockeyed the Ski-Doos and the sleds into position, tied our loads behind us. John started up, and we formed a line behind him.

Our big, overloaded Nansen sleds, with the rolled-up yellow tents strapped on top, looked like a string of Conestoga wagons. As we set out, I started humming the refrain of "Westward Ho" to myself, and kept a lookout for Comanches.

It was cold. Traveling crosswise to the wind also meant traveling crosswise to the sastrugi, the ridges of snow that paralleled the direction of the prevailing wind. It meant a bumpy ride.

The blowing snow held down visibility. Coming from my right, it also meant that half of me was significantly colder than the other half. And the windward side was also the side of my throttle hand. I stopped to switch gloves, putting my heavy leather glove on the dashboard and replacing it with an even heavier bear claw glove. At some point in the trip, the glove on the dashboard blew away, and I never even noticed it.

But the worst was the big sled hitched up behind me. Tall and top heavy, it had more sail area facing the wind than a Tech Dinghy, and like a dinghy it had no keel to stop it from capsizing. Between the wind and the bumpy surface, it was a prime candidate for tipping over.

Which it did.

Seven times.

And it was too big to tip back on my own. That meant stopping the whole train, at least once an hour, and waiting for help.

It didn't help matters that John was clearly eager to get home and tended to race on ahead of us. The train stretched out over maybe half a mile; at times, with the blowing snow, I lost track of our leader entirely. Trying to keep up with the sleds in front of me, I would lose contact with the people behind me. At times I'd have a 10-minute wait, in the cold and blowing snow, before someone would come along to help me tip my sled back up.

I got the feeling that Ralph and René were getting sick of helping me out. I knew I was getting sick of it. After 6 weeks of dirty looks from them, emphasizing my incompetence at just about everything on the ice, this was the final indignity.

All right . . . so I didn't have Ralph's strength or experience. I didn't have René's energy. I didn't have Sara's or Laurie's ability to recognize meteorite types (especially since, with my eyesight, I could barely see them). I wasn't a professional mountain guide like John. But geez, couldn't these people appreciate my special talents? Like . . . like . . .

Driving through the snow, I was hard pressed to come up with any.

Driving a snowmobile? As my sled teetered over for the umpteenth time, I let that one pass.

Cooking? Ralph did all of that.

Sharing stories, or books, or music? Nobody seemed to have my taste in those.

Serving as an example of gentle living and good humor under extreme conditions? Yeah, right . . . I was the guy playing mind games with my tentmate for a week.

Feeling low and useless, I drove on. The snow piled up against the side of my parka. The Antarctic plateau on a windy cold day was a great place for a self-pity jag.

It did get easier, toward the end. Traveling downwind, on softer snow, we finally began to make good time. Then, suddenly, John stopped and we all pulled up beside him. Puzzled, I got off my Ski-Doo to find out what was happening.

"You don't recognize it?" he asked, waving his arm at a featureless flat field of white. "This is it."

Not too far away, I finally saw a pile of boxes and metal pallets. We were back at Griffin.

Of course, that meant another hour of setting up tents, putting down the floors, getting things ready to spend a couple of nights. Ralph seemed even more distant than usual. I tried my best to help out, but it seemed I could do little right. Finally I just tried my best to stay out of his way.

The next day was snowy and cold, and we were exhausted. Ralph and John announced that work was postponed until the afternoon; that was fine with me.

But the afternoon had plenty to keep us busy. The pile of pallets and boxes had been surrounded by drifting snow; they had to be shoveled out, dragged up to the level of the current surface, and then loaded up. I slowly caught on to the method of piling up boxes and strapping nets over them. There was plenty of work to keep us all busy.

But again, that night was a quiet, somber dinner.

Part of it, I learned, was John's anxiety about the weather. "Do you know any good prayers?" he asked me. "If it doesn't clear up tomorrow, we could be stuck here for another week."

"Well, there's that blue-ice field to the north of here we always wanted to take a look at," Ralph suggested. The rest of us groaned.

Feeling more than a bit foolish, a bit like the chaplain in the movie *Patton* who's ordered to pray for attacking weather, I talked to God that night. Maybe, I decided, they'd found one thing for me to do that I wouldn't totally screw up.

Sunlight and clouds played tag in the sky the next morning. John radioed in the weather, and learned that it was, for the moment, not too bad in McMurdo, either.

"But will it hold?" he asked me, skeptically. I shrugged.

"You ordered sunshine," I answered.

A storm was threatening for the whole area, McMurdo informed him. But they'd send at least one Herc flight out for half of us.

It arrived an hour later. The Navy crew, new people to talk to, were a sight for cold eyes. John dragged pallets to the back of their plane, they attached ropes and winched them up the back, while we tugged and lifted corners to get them loaded.

Two of the tents were down and packed. Only John and René would be hanging back, waiting for the second flight . . . should it come. Finally, fully loaded, we were instructed to board the front of the plane. Avoiding the props, which had been kept churning the entire time the plane was on the snow, we climbed aboard.

As I strapped myself into the seat, I began to calculate. This was my third trip by Herc. In both the previous cases, the trips had been aborted once before we finally got on our way. Would this happen again?

"The trip off the ice was the scariest part of my last season," Sara had informed us, a month ago. Her words came back to haunt me. "The plane couldn't take off, and they had to dump half of our stuff back on the ice before we could get off the ground," she'd said.

Now the engines roared into life, and we slowly, slowly, began to bump across the snow.

Ralph did not look encouraged. "It's not very windy today," he said. "We may not be able to get up to take-off speed."

And we bumped. And bumped. And bumped.

"I think we're going to taxi back to McMurdo," he shouted. Except for the Transantarctic Mountains in our way, it didn't seem like a bad idea. "We must be a quarter of the way back to where we were on Christmas by now."

The Navy crew looked tight-lipped. I started praying again.

"Two miles so far," one of the Navy crew passed back from the cockpit.

We hit a big bump, bigger than before, that shook the plane. Then a thud, as we hit the snow. Then another big bump . . .

"He's looking for—" Ralph started to shout.

But we could hear, and feel, the difference. As one of the bumps launched us into the air, just momentarily, the plane was no longer being dragged back by the ice beneath its skids. For a moment at least it could lurch forward, just a bit faster . . . just fast enough to keep off the ground. The longer we stayed airborne—counting in seconds—the faster we could get going. And finally, this time, we were airborne for good.

We heard, later, about the extra adventure that John and René experienced. By the time our crew had dropped us off and returned from McMurdo, the weather conditions had worsened considerably. I guess I'd only asked for enough blue sky to get me home; or maybe God had it in for René and his skepticism! In any event, the Herc crew were facing classic white-out conditions. With no blue sky, there was no visible horizon . . . and no way of telling how far below them the ground was. Coasting downwind, past the camp, the crew was about to radio to John and René the bad news, that landing had become impossible and they were likely stuck on the ice, by themselves, for another week or so. Just before slowly banking into a turn, however, the plane suffered a sudden and unexpected jolt.

"Well," said the pilot, "I guess we're landing after all." And they slowly taxied back, up wind, to the camp and the waiting campers.

Meanwhile, Ralph and Sara and Laurie and I were on the ground in McMurdo. Since we'd left, the ice shelf had thinned enough that planes could no longer land there; in another month, the supply ship would actually be afloat on water there. So instead we'd landed at the summer airfield a few miles away from McMurdo, Williams Field. It was a long ride from "Willie" in an overheated snow bus, past the New Zealand base, down by the thinning ice where now we could see seals sunning themselves, and across the volcanic rock. It felt good to be home, and yet . . .

"This is always the worst time of the trip for me," Ralph said to Laurie, sitting across from me. "It's the time when I know I have to let John make the decisions, and you know how hard it is for me to let somebody else run things. But even worse, I get the feeling I can't do anything right."

He sighed. My ears perked up. Ralph felt that way, too? Ralph?

"I mean," he continued, "John will say, 'Paint this box green,' so I'll paint it green, and then he'll come back and ask, 'why did you do that? I told you to paint it purple,' and everyone else around me will agree, that's what he said. I just feel so totally incompetent and use-less . . ."

He was talking to Laurie, only to Laurie. But I realized, and he must have realized, that Sara and I were listening, too. He was really saying, "It's OK. You guys did good. You wish you could have done more? We all wish that. But we're back, and we're safe, no one's hurt, no one's mad at you . . .

"And we have 390 new specimens from outer space sitting in a box back at the airport, waiting to be shipped off to Houston."

That was, after all, what I'd gone to Antarctica for.

Wasn't it?

AFTERWORD—
ABOUT THIS BOOK

ACK IN the relative peace of the Specola Vaticana, the Alban Hills rolling and blue with summer's haze outside my window, I return from a two-week retreat of prayer and self-reflection to the demands of my laptop. I have mail. Lots of mail. But book's done, the manuscript is safely in the capable hands of my editors, and now I have the time to answer some of those e-mail messages.

I'm worried that, once the book is published, there could be a flurry of e-mail from folks wanting to know more—about me, the Vatican Observatory, and the book itself. In anticipation of such questions, I offer the following Q & A session. I hope that it will provide some of the answers my readers will be looking for.

Or at least, deflect a few of those e-mails!

So where's the hot and juicy gossip about the Vatican?
I don't know any. And even if I did, why would I spill it all in a book? I have never really understood those people who have to live vicariously on the scandal and excitement of someone else's life.

And the fact is, most of the sorts of things that the tabloid editors are looking for just aren't to be found. There are no conspiracies to hide evidence of extraterrestrials. There is no secret asteroid-about-to-destroy-civilization. (Why would any astronomer keep it secret? Think of the fame and glory, not to mention the increase in funding, that would come with such a discovery!)

Nor is there an "office" at the Vatican in charge of extraterrestrial affairs, or anything else of that ilk.

But surely someone at the Vatican is worried about all that sort of stuff?
No. And why should they be?

I think too many people see "the Vatican" as a big mysterious organization of wise but secretive wizards ready to issue a proclamation, or at least a press statement, on any and every event in human history. The truth is more embarrassing . . . that the few people who really do work at the Vatican have far more interesting issues to worry about. Like the state of ordinary people's lives.

Likewise, those unfamiliar with science tend to glamorize it, either to deify or demonize it. Trust me, some of my best friends are scientists . . . and we aren't that smart. As they say at NASA, it doesn't take a rocket scientist to be a rocket scientist.

It may be—and I am only speculating—that the discussion of extraterrestrial life following the ALH 84001 Mars-rock discoveries could have figured in Pope John Paul II's statement in 1996, affirming evolution as "more than just a hypothesis" which theologians should take seriously. But certainly that would have been only one small element in his thinking. And that's just about the only example I can think of for a kind of direct Pope/space link. (Though, when we showed him our images of Comet Shoemaker-Levy impacting into

Jupiter, which we had observed from Castel Gandolfo, he did kindly say, "Bless you; and bless your comets!")

He's interested . . . but only as we all are interested.

You mean nobody at the Vatican cares about the possibility of life on Mars?

I can only think of one person at the Vatican who officially has anything to do with Mars. Me. And I'm a scientist, not a theologian. Because whether there is life on another planet or not is a scientific question, not a religious one. It's all one universe; all the same Creator. He could have created any way He wanted. The fun is in finding out which, of the many possible ways, He actually chose.

I'm also surprised you don't talk about telescopes more. Don't you ever use a telescope?

I'll spend several weeks a year on the mountain, observing. It's a peaceful, indeed almost a monastic experience. But it's hard to tell stories about it. Like a monastery, from the outside the daily life can seem quite tedious. Think about novels set in medieval monasteries (the Brother Cadfael mysteries are a favorite) and you'll realize how little of the action actually takes place within the cloister.

So if there's nothing in here about the Vatican, and nothing startling seen through a telescope, then why did you write this book?

The publisher invited me to. And I agreed. Not for the money; it goes to the Observatory, not to me. Not for the glory; as my religious superior in our Tucson community, Father Murphy, reassured me, "Don't worry, Guy, you have plenty of things to keep you humble!"

And not because I am particularly unusual compared to other scientists, either by being smarter or being more religious. But what is unusual is that I am *publicly* religious, with a formal education in theology and philosophy as well as the hard sciences. Where most other scientists, rightly I think, consider their religious beliefs to be private and nobody's business, I am in a position both by training and by my assignment from the Jesuits to talk publicly about things those scientists hold privately.

Indeed, I doubt that there is anything in this book that would surprise or disturb either a scientist or a theologian. I just happen to be in a position to say it out loud.

I chose the topics in this book because over the years they're the topics I have been asked about, repeatedly. In fact, several of these chapters are based on talks I have given, or articles I have written, over the past few years.

Can you be more specific?

The Introduction, "A Day in the Life," first appeared in a slightly shorter form as "Brother Astronomer" in the December 1998 issue of the National Space Society magazine *Ad Astra*.

"A Vindication of Mars" is based on a talk given at the Excellence in Science Education award luncheon in Houston in 1999.

Most of "Precursors of Evil" was presented at the conference "Myth and Magic in the Sky" in 1997. The quotations from the works of Grassi, Galileo, and their students are adapted from the translations of Stillman Drake and Charles Donald O'Malley, found in *The Controversy on the Comets of 1618,* University of Pennsylvania Press (1960). Details on the life of Grassi come from the book *Galileo, for Copernicanism and for the Church* by Annibale Fantoli (Vatican Observatory Publications, 1994, revised 1996).

Parts of "The Rift of Popular Culture" were presented as a talk at the St. Albert the Great Forum of the University of Arizona, itself based in part on a paper, "Astronomy, Science Fiction and Popular Culture: 1277 to 2001 (and Beyond)" which appeared in the journal *Leonardo,* volume 29, pp. 127–132, in February 1996; and on the introduction to another book of mine, *The Way to the Dwelling of Light,* published by the Vatican Observatory (distributed outside Italy by the University of Notre Dame Press) in 1998.

The quotations from the writings of Athansius in the chapter "Finding God in Creation" are my attempt at an idiomatic translation of *On the Incarnation,* based on the translation of St. Vladimir's Seminary Press, 1944. The quotes from John Eriugena are a slightly edited version of the translation by I. P. Sheldon-Williams, Dublin Institute for Advanced Studies, 1981.

Parts of "Wide Wild Whiteness" have appeared in the Spring 1999 issue of *Company* and the April 1999 issue of *Meteorite!*

Finally, note that all scripture quotations are from the New Revised Standard Version of the Bible, ©1989 by the Division of Christian Education of the National Council of Churches of Christ in the United States. All rights reserved. Used by permission.

Is there anyone in particular you would like to acknowledge?

My editors at McGraw-Hill, Griffin Hansbury and Amy Murphy, did a superb job of keeping this book on track through the whole production process. And, unlike the trend in too many publishers, they actually edited this book. Ruthlessly! What merit there is in it, they dragged out of me.

The late Father Dick Polakowski, SJ, was my high school English teacher; Jim Fitzgerald, the now-retired feature columnist with the *Detroit Free Press,* was my editor at the Lapeer (Michigan) *County Press.* They taught me how to write. My father, himself a journalist, taught me how to be a writer. (There's a difference.) I thank them all.

Cliff Stoll, who gave me the laptop computer I used when I wrote this book—thanks, Cliff!

Darryl Kent, Amtrak steward on the Texas Eagle, kept me happy and sane during a cross-country train trip from Tucson to New York, when I did most of my editing and rewriting; smiles and cheers to him!

And to all the people who couldn't reach me by phone or e-mail that week . . . how do you think I ever got this book written?

About the Author

Born in Detroit, a classic baby-boomer child of the Sputnik age, Brother Guy Consolmagno was interested in rockets and astronomy from childhood. He first encountered the Jesuits in high school, from whom he learned history, Latin, Greek, and the rest of intellectual life outside of rockets and astronomy. For the next 20 years, he vacillated between a life in astronomy and with the Jesuits, earning bachelor's and master's degrees in science from MIT, and a Ph.D. in planetary science from the University of Arizona, while still staying active in his parish and keeping in touch with Jesuit friends. In 1983, he left a post-doctoral research position at MIT to join the Peace Corps, serving in Kenya for two years—teaching astronomy. Finally, in 1989, Consolmagno entered the Jesuit order, taking vows as a brother in 1991 and being assigned to the Vatican as an astronomer in 1993. At the Vatican, Consolmagno serves as curator of the meteorite collection, one of the largest in the world, and does research on the physical evolution of meteorites. He also observes asteroids, comets, and small moons with the Vatican's Advanced Technology Telescope (VATT) at the Vatican's observatory in Arizona. His other books include *Turn Left at Orion*, with Dan Davis, a book for beginning amateurs on how to use a small telescope; *Worlds Apart*, with Martha Schaefer, a planetary sciences textbook; and *The Way to the Dwelling of Light*, a book on modern physics for religious laymen. He has most recently contributed to *Cosmic Pinball*, a book that explores the science of comets, meteors, and asteroids. Brother Guy Consolmagno lives in Tucson, Arizona, and at Castel Gandolfo, just outside of Rome.

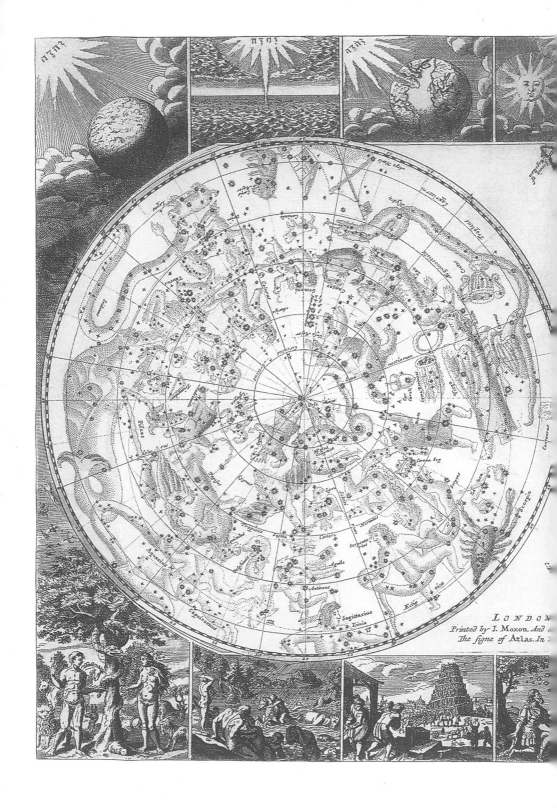

LONDON
Printed by I. Moxon. And a
The signe of Atlas. In